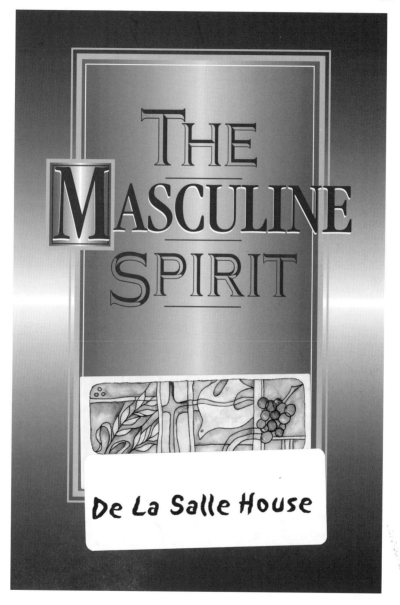

THE MASCULINE SPIRIT

De La Salle House

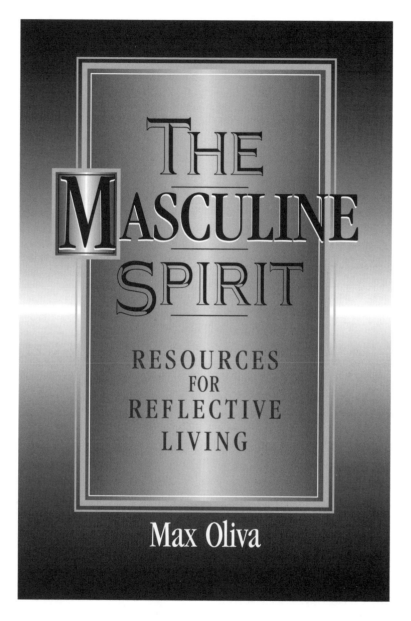

THE MASCULINE SPIRIT

RESOURCES FOR REFLECTIVE LIVING

Max Oliva

AVE MARIA PRESS Notre Dame, Indiana 46556

© 1997 by Ave Maria Press, Inc.

Cover and text design by Katherine Robinson Coleman

Printed and bound in the United States of America.

Library of Congress Cataloging-in-Publication Data

Oliva, Max.
        The masculine spirit : resources for reflective living
  / Max Oliva.
         p.   cm.
    Includes bibliographical references.
    ISBN 0-87793-630-7
        1. Men—Religious life. 2. Christian life—Catholic
authors. 3. Masculinity—Religious aspects—Christianity. 4.
Archetype (Psychology) 5. Men—Psychology. I. Title.
     BV4528.2.O45   1997
     248.8'42—dc21
                                    97-20164
                                        CIP

Contents

To REFLECT: to think, to ponder, or meditate; to reflect on one's virtues and faults.

REFLECTION: a fixing of the thoughts on something; careful consideration.

REFLECTIVE: given to or concerned with meditation.

—*Random House Dictionary*

*In memory of my father and mother
and my grandparents.*

To those men and women
who have taught me
what it means to be
a true King, Warrior,
Magician, and Lover.

ACKNOWLEDGMENTS

I am grateful to a number of people who helped make this book possible:

Thirteen male friends who took time to reflect carefully and write out their feelings and thoughts on some key life issues, such as work, intimacy, prayer, and play. Their stories have challenged and inspired me. They are Joe Baxter, Tom Collart, Steve Faucher, Gary Glasheen, Dave Hokanson, Dick Lennon, John O'Reilly, Earl Parrish, Mario Renda, Carl Smith, Mike Smith, Len Smorin, and Terry Swagerty.

A number of men who, through informal conversation, assisted in my research for the book: Doug Bacon, Bill Jones, Bob Raspo, Don Small, Kevin Smith, Frank Thornton, and Maurile Tremblay.

Men I have met on retreats that I have given, who have shared from their hearts, especially, Bob Bixel, George Brunz, Liam Cluskey, Ken Eckel, Vito Elarde, Jack Flannery, Dick Gossman, Jack Hawkes, Herb Ibarra, and Larry Powell.

The Jesuits with whom I live—Fathers Richard Brown, Jaimie Rasura, and Augusto Berrio—for their inspiration, encouragement, and support.

Women friends who support me by helping me to develop the anima dimension of my personality. The Religious of the Sacred Heart Sisters of Ocean Beach, California, with whom I am privileged to pray on a regular basis. In particular for Sister Mary Ann Foy, who has been an excellent spiritual guide for eight years.

Frank Cunningham, publisher of Ave Maria Press, whose idea it was to begin this writing project. And, last but far from least, my editor and friend, Bob Hamma, for his insightful suggestions and gentle way of challenging me to improve the text where needed.

To all the above, I am most grateful and wish the fullness of God's blessing.

Introduction

Many men are confused today about what it is to be a man. Some are even embarrassed about being male. There are questions of identity, role, and what positive contributions men can make to the family and to the world.

This is a book to help men value themselves, to own and celebrate the beneficial characteristics of masculinity while at the same time rejecting false images of being male. Men and women are created to be in a partnership, neither one dominating the other, each using their God-given gifts of gender for the benefit of the other and for the redemption of the planet.

To help men discover more fully the true masculine mode of being, I have chosen to treat extensively the art of reflection. I have personally experienced the benefits of living a reflective life and know that this is the way to maturity and wholeness. This is the way to become aware of wounds from our childhood, some of which trap us into unhealthy behavior as adults. This is the way to learn from our mistakes so that we are not doomed to keep repeating them. This is the way to discover the positive traits of what it is to be a man.

As an overall format for considering the practice of reflection, this book will present the four basic male archetypes—King, Warrior, Magician, and Lover—and explain and illustrate them with lively stories. Archetypes are blueprints, primordial images, that affect how we think, feel, and react to life's situations. Each archetype has both positive and negative characteristics. Reflecting on these has helped me (and others) to better understand myself, to own the good and discard the bad.

Each of us were influenced, for better or for worse, by our father and mother, or another significant adult figure. Unfortunately, the bad effects do not just disappear when we become adults; they emerge in sometimes destructive behavior in our roles as husbands, fathers, and bosses. The adverse influences need to be faced and owned if we are to be healed of them. The art of reflecting is the necessary tool for this process.

While the ability to reflect on our experiences in order to learn from them is a gift from God, it is also a skill we can learn. I have seen this learning take place time and again in the many retreats I give. In the book, I want to share how I came to be a reflective person and suggest a variety of tools that you can use as well.

Every aspect of our lives gives us the opportunity to practice the art of reflection. For me, as for many men, my relationship with my father was an area of my life very much in need of reflection and healing. In Chapter Seven, I relate how, through reflection, I was progressively healed of emotional wounds I received from my father. In other parts of the book, I relate the positive contributions my father handed on to me.

There are many important life issues that call us to reflect. I asked twelve male friends from the United States and Ireland to share their feelings and thoughts, as men, on seven key issues: work, play, intimacy, prayer, networking, transition to retirement (for those who have retired), and ultimate concerns. With their permission, I have included a number of their written reflections in the book. Their stories illustrate the value and the benefits of reflecting on one's life.[1]

There are questions for reflection at the conclusion of each of the chapters on the male archetypes. In the final chapter some of the techniques for reflection mentioned briefly in earlier chapters are treated more fully.

As a Jesuit, I have been profoundly influenced by the spirituality of St. Ignatius of Loyola and by his Spiritual Exercises, a series of reflections on his experiences of God that is presented in a retreat format. Writing this book put me in touch, on a deeper level, with many of Ignatius' insights, and helped me to discover the fullness of the King, Warrior, Magician, and Lover in Jesus Christ. It is my hope that you will have a similar experience, that through this book you will not only discover important truths about yourself, but about the Son of God as well.

ONE

Beginnings

Do not look back in anger
nor forward in fear
but around in awareness.

—James Thurber

I grew up in the 40s and 50s, in an upwardly mobile, middle-class family. My father was a businessman, a salesman, who, following World War II, started a food brokerage company in Los Angeles. My mother, in addition to raising a family of five children and doing household chores, generously spent some of her time reaching out to those in our church community who were in need of food and clothing. Both my father and mother were faithful Catholics. They attended Mass every Sunday and made sure their children received a good Catholic education.

I left home at the age of twenty-one, after graduating from college with a bachelors degree in marketing, to sow a few wild oats before settling down with my father in the family business. At least that was the plan. I traveled in Europe for four months. I was in Berlin eight days after the wall went up, ran with the bulls in Pamplona, in the annual San Fermin Festival, and, in general, came into contact with a world vastly different from the one in which I had been raised. Shortly after returning home, I enlisted in the United States Coast Guard, serving in a special reserves program for college graduates: six months active duty, seven-and-a-half years of reserves. Active duty put me in close contact with a wider diversity of men than I had known at home or in college whose religious beliefs and practices varied a great deal from mine. Like my time in Europe, the Coast Guard had a maturing effect on me, though I was not aware of this until later.

Upon completion of the active component of military service, I returned to school to study for a masters in business administration. However, I ran out of money after one semester and so accepted an offer to work as a salesman for a food cannery. Like the possible M.B.A., this job seemed good preparation for eventually joining my father in his business, a venture I did not yet feel ready to undertake.

When I look back on these early experiences, I realize I was not a reflective person. Events happened, and I went with them. I did not think much about who I was or where I was going, except in general terms of eventual marriage, family, and so forth.

What I did have, though, was a quiet side to my personality. I liked to walk in the hills near where I lived, to read novels, and to have lunch in a park near the cannery. I usually brought a book to read. In the tranquil setting of rose bushes and shady trees, I would be refreshed for the afternoon business.

Though I was successful as a salesman, I felt disillusioned at times by the lack of ethical behavior I saw in some of my coworkers: overcharging on travel expenses, drinking to excess during lunches, and occasionally not giving our customers the quality of product they had ordered. Not that I was a saint, but my moral lapses mainly occurred outside the work place. There I was living a fast-paced life, giving and going to lots of parties, driving a speedy sports car: going through my "prodigal" time, as it were. Attendance at Sunday Mass took a beating as did other devotions I had learned from my parents. But gradually, it began to dawn on me that something was missing in my life though I did not know what. Perhaps it was a sense of meaning.[1]

Sometimes it takes a miracle to wake us up to the deeper purpose of life. You meet the right person, fall in love, and settle down in marriage. Or you and your wife have your first child and suddenly things that seemed so important before pale in significance in the face of this new person, a veritable extension of yourself. My miracle came two months into the twenty-fourth year of my life. That is when I realized that deep down in my heart I wanted to be a priest. A Jesuit priest.

Miracles are unpredictable. And, as I was to discover, untraceable. In the space of one month after I thought about joining the Jesuits, I entered the Jesuit novitiate.[2] I quit my job, gave all my earthly possessions into the care of my father, including my beloved sports car, and left the bachelor lifestyle. Joining the Jesuits was a giant leap of faith and I was not sure I had made the right decision until the second week in my new home. I received a grace from God that confirmed this is where I belonged. As I mentioned above, while working at the cannery and pursuing a playboy way of life, I felt unfulfilled at some deep level. It was like I was at loose ends within. In this moment of grace, all the loose ends came together, a profound peace descended, and I knew without a doubt that this is where I wanted to be.

For the first couple of months in the novitiate I tried to figure out how all this had happened. It was such an unexpected and swift change, from the business world to religious life. This was probably my first real try at reflecting on life. With hindsight I could perceive some arrows that pointed in the direction of turning my life around, but the full extent of the change was pure mystery. I could not make logical sense of it. Yet I knew without a doubt that I had made the right decision.

I now had a sense of meaning and a purpose to my life. I came across Francis Thompson's marvelous poem, "The Hound of Heaven," in the novitiate library. It provided me with valuable insight about what had been going on for the previous four or five years, especially in the following lines:

I fled Him, down the nights and down the days;
I fled Him, down the arches of the years;
I fled Him, down the labyrinthine ways
of my own mind; and in the mist of tears
I hid from Him, and under running laughter.
Up vistaed hopes, I sped;
And shot, precipitated,
Adown Titanic gloom of chasmed fears,
From those strong Feet that followed,
followed after.[3]

A few years later I was to find a passage in St. Paul's Letter to the Philippians that shed new light on my vocation and what I had left behind.

But those things I used to consider gain I have now reappraised as loss in the light of Christ. I have come to rate all as loss in the surpassing knowledge of my Lord Jesus Christ. (3:7-8 NAB)

Christ had become the Center of my life. I found in him that which I had been searching for.

Another section from "The Hound of Heaven" explained what had happened from God's perspective:

All which I took from thee I did but take,
Not for thy harms,
But just that thou might'st seek it in My arms.

All which thy child's mistake
Fancies as lost, I have stored for thee at home:
Rise, clasp My hand, and come.[4]

The Art of Reflecting

In his book, *The Heart's Journey Home*, Nicholas Harnan gives four suggestions to promote the art of reflective living:

- Slow down; that is, cultivate a slower rhythm in one's daily life;

- Reconnect with a deeper order in reality, an order beyond one's immediate control;

- Stay with an experience in order to discern its deeper meaning and resist all urges to try to manipulate it;

- Share one's thoughts and feelings with a trusted companion.[5]

These four steps summarize what was occurring in my life as I made the transition from life as a salesman to life as a Jesuit novice. But one need not change his lifestyle so radically to become a reflective person. As we begin our exploration of how to become more reflective within the context of our busy lives and many commitments, these steps can be very helpful.

Slowing Down

Doug, a firefighter, is in his mid-forties. He is a husband and father of three sons. Recently, he related to me how he slows down in order to keep in touch with his basic values.

When I come home from a shift at work, I am usually so tired I go right to sleep. But at the station, at twilight time, as I lie awake in bed I reflect on my life. I consider how my family is doing, how I'm treating my wife and kids, on whether or not we have all our bills paid. I think about myself and how I act towards the people I meet in my work. Sometimes I encounter heart-breaking situations. I wonder if I'm doing enough good deeds for others, you know, spontaneous good acts. I believe one act of goodness towards someone multiplies the good in the world as they, in turn, help someone else.

Sometimes the circumstances of life force us to reduce our pace. The loss of a job, an illness, or a serious accident gives us unexpected time on our hands that can lead to new insights about our life if we take advantage of this free time. Even retirement can lead to more reflective time as the following stories illustrate.

Dick worked for thirty-two years in the area of personnel for a public utility corporation. He relates: "I have been retired for three years and I find this to be the most satisfying period of my life. My days are filled with physical activity, study, recreation, travel, and spiritual activities as well as quiet periods for contemplative prayer."

Frank is a retired school principal. Occasionally he finds himself in his den reminiscing about his life. He gazes at the pictures on the walls, photos of family and friends spanning many years, and thanks God for the blessings he has received. He considers various objects in the room that he has collected since he was a young man and lets his memory drift back to both the happy and the sad times.

This is a deliberate act of slowing down for Frank because as he sheepishly admits, "I am busier now than before I retired!"

There are many ways to reflect and a variety of places to do so. What is needed most is the *will* to take the time, to realize that such an exercise can improve one personally, professionally, and spiritually.

Richard is the CEO of a state-wide utility company. He sets aside some eight hours each week for solitary reflection. He walks, works in his basement shop, or rides his Harley. He says, "You have to force yourself to spend some time away from the hustle and bustle of your job in order to get down to reality again. If you don't spend enough time doing that, you can lose hold of the reins and get into all kinds of trouble."[6]

Where is that special place of quiet for you, where you are able to slow down? Is it on an airplane while on a business trip? Or in your car when you deliberately leave the radio or cassette player off? Do you find yourself sifting through your feelings and thoughts while taking a leisurely walk, or when jogging or swimming? Perhaps you find the quiet in your own backyard or at a nearby park, at a serene spot on the farm or at your favorite fishing hole. Some find peace at the beach, others, in the desert, by a lake, or on a mountain peak. Still others, in their church. And, some find slow-down time in their home, by the fire on a cold winter night or, like Frank, in their study or den.

We learn from the gospels that Jesus was aware of the need to take time out of a busy schedule for rest and relaxation. Mark relates how he sent the apostles out two by two to preach, to expel demons, and to cure the sick. When they returned from their ministry full of excitement at the wonderful things that had happened but tired from their activities, Jesus said to them, "Let us go off by ourselves to some place where we will be alone and you can rest awhile" (Mark 6:31).

Jesus also said to his disciples, "Come to me, all of you who are tired from carrying heavy loads, and I will give you rest" (Matthew 11:28). "Heavy loads" can represent stress, anxieties, financial concerns, anything which disturbs our peace of mind. Jesus' invitation to take a break came to me once in an unexpected way. It happened at the time I was working at the cannery. One day, on the way home from work, I stopped at the local Catholic church in the town where I lived. I felt the need to go to confession. As I sat in the pew saying my penance after seeing the priest, my attention was caught by the color of the wall behind the altar. It was a pleasant blue. I felt very much at peace, gazing at it. Interesting, I wasn't thinking about Jesus being in the Blessed Sacrament; it was the color of the wall that soothed me. I recall returning to that church often on my way home from work, just to sit there and enjoy the peace.

St. Luke tells us that Mary, Jesus' mother, had a habit of pondering significant events in her life and in the life of her family. After the birth of Jesus and the surprise visit by the shepherds, Luke writes, "Mary treasured all these things and reflected on them in her heart" (Luke 2:19 NAB). To accentuate this practice of hers, Luke reiterates the sentiment when he tells us, in verse 51 of the same chapter, that Mary pondered Jesus staying behind in Jerusalem, at the age of twelve, to try to make sense of his action. To reflect in your heart on your experience implies a slowing down. Only then can you hear your inner voice and the promptings of the Holy Spirit and find the answers you seek.

There are many ways to express the benefits of cultivating a slower rhythm. The Irish poet, William Butler Yeats, found his peace of soul in a special setting. He wrote of this in the beautiful, reflective poem, "The Lake Isle of Innisfree:"

> I will arise and go now, and go to Innisfree,
> And a small cabin build there, of clay and wattles
>   made:
> Nine bean-rows will I have there, a hive for the
>   honeybee,
> And live alone in the bee-loud glade.
>
> And I shall have some peace there, for peace comes
>   dropping slow,
> Dropping from the veils of the morning to where the
>   cricket sings;
> There midnight's all a glimmer, and noon a purple
>   glow,
> And evening full of the linnet's wings.
>
> I will arise and go now, for always night and day
> I hear lake water lapping with low sounds by the
>   shore;
> While I stand on the roadway, or on the pavements
>   grey,
> I hear it in the deep heart's core.[7]

Reconnecting

Harnan's second step to promote the art of reflective living is to reconnect with a deeper order in reality, an order beyond our immediate control. Sometimes the act of reconnecting comes in the form of self-searching.

Tom is forty-eight years old, a husband and father. His job involves a great deal of responsibility and performance pressure, but also provides rewards in terms of recognition within his company and a good salary. Yet he finds himself' concerned about his vulnerability in the job market. He tells of this in his own words:

> One of the issues that seem to be most troubling to me now is a struggle with the quest for security in this world: the economy, job security, maintaining my standard of living. I would like someday to work at a different job, one which is more service-oriented to those in need, but I don't know if I'll get the opportunity. Is it a chance that I should take, I ask myself, if doing so involves financial risk? I am now in my late forties and the idea of getting older is not really troubling except I wonder if when my life is done I will have accomplished the things I should have.
>
> I probably judge myself by a more stringent standard than I apply to others, but I do wonder, "Am I doing the things I should?" "Am I nurturing my faith adequately?" "Have I let my conscience become too arbitrary?" It seems there are a lot fewer moral absolutes now than when I was twenty or thirty. The Catholic Church herself seems to be having some of the same problems as I am and as a result does not provide the same security she once did. I believe that God is in control and is using my experiences, anxieties, and joys to provide guidance. I don't always get the message, but God has blessed me with the faith to know that he loves me enough to keep the communication going.

The avenues toward reconnecting with a deeper order in reality are many, though some can be scary: a recession, down-sizing, plant closures, or company takeovers can force us to re-think our values. Sometimes an unanticipated event results in a long struggle to recapture a sense of meaning in our life. Such was the situation for Joe.

Joe is from Northern Ireland, is a Catholic, and was fifteen years old when the Troubles began. Here is part of his story. He is recounting his struggle with finding meaning in his work:

Over the years I have become more at ease with the notion that work is a wholesome, necessary, even essential part of life. Alas, things were not always this way. Upon reflection, I now realize that for years I suffered a feeling of having been robbed of my dream. I was to have been a professional soccer player for a team in England at the age of sixteen, until an unfortunate encounter with British troops and the police changed my life. So, instead of my life-long dream coming true, I ended up an employee for the city water department. Until I was in my early thirties, I felt that my job was an unimportant, necessary evil, something I had to do to provide for my wife and children.

A few years ago I made a weekend retreat. During one of the prayer periods, the question of work came into my mind. A passage from the Bible was disclosed to me. It said, "Work as unto the Lord." That was the beginning of my process of change. I suddenly realized how negative my thinking had been about my job and how emotionally damaging this had been for me. Following the retreat, my work improved, my relationships with my bosses got better, and my self-esteem grew. Occasionally my dream comes back to haunt me, but I now know that you are never too old to dream new dreams.

Once in a while, when we are in a moment of vulnerability, a certain author touches us with words of consolation that help us to connect with a deeper order in reality. A few years ago, in the space of two months, I experienced three significant losses: the death of my father, the selling of our family home, and the unexpected loss of the diocesan parish I had been living in for three enriching years. I was in a state of emotional and spiritual upheaval. Grief for my losses and uncertainty as to where I would live tormented me. Since my main ministry is giving retreats, I live "in residence," that is, I pay room and board. There are only two Jesuit houses in San Diego and, at that time, they were both full. I didn't know where I would go and felt uprooted. During the time I was at my lowest ebb, a friend gave me a book called, *The Joy of Full Surrender.* The following paragraph brought meaning to what I was experiencing.

> To live by faith is to live by joy, confidence, and certainty about all that has to be done or suffered at each moment by God's will. It is in order to animate and to maintain this life of faith that God allows us to be plunged into and carried away by the rough waters of numerous pains, troubles, difficulties, weaknesses, and defeats. For *it requires faith to find God in all these* (emphasis mine). The divine life is given to us at every moment in a hidden but very sure way, under different appearances. . . . [8]

I have also found Psalm 27 to be an excellent prayer when things get out of control and I need to be reminded that beyond the external appearances is the Rock of my salvation.

> The Lord is my light and my salvation;
> I will fear no one.
> The Lord protects me from all danger;
> I will never be afraid.

Trust in the Lord.
Have faith, do not despair.
Trust in the Lord (Ps 27:1, 14).

Staying with an Experience

The third step in promoting a reflective lifestyle is to stay with an experience, be it painful or pleasant, in order to discover its deeper meaning. This means going beyond denial and overcoming the temptation to manipulate the experience.

I must confess that of the four steps, this one is the most difficult for me. I resist pain. Either I try to wish it away, or I seek escape from it. This is equally true whether the pain is physical, mental, emotional, or spiritual. I remember my novice master telling me that I would have to pray in the future for what he called, "a love of the cross." He was right. Sometimes I have found the strength to go through a difficult situation by contemplating the second Station of the Cross where Jesus takes upon himself his cross. I ask God that I may have Jesus' disposition, a willingness to carry my own cross. I then discover the courage to do so. Recently, I came across a helpful image for staying with unpleasant feelings. The Chinese character for patience (Jen) shows a knife poised over a heart. It signifies the willingness to hold still in painful settings, until we know what we are feeling.[9]

In his book, *Fire in the Belly: On Being a Man*, Sam Keen describes the Soulful Quest, or pilgrimage into self, that a man must make if he is to find his true masculine self. To go on this journey demands staying with a variety of inner experiences. Keen explains:

> The Soulful Quest is a pilgrimage into the depths of the self. We leave the sunlit world of easy roles and prefabricated tokens of masculinity, penetrate the character armor, get beneath the personality and plunge into the chaos and pain of the old "masculine" self. This isn't the fun part of the trip. It's

spelunking in Plato's cave, feeling our way through the illusions we have mistaken for reality, crawling through the drain sewers where the forbidden "unmanly" feelings dwell, confronting the demons and dark shadows that have held us captive from their underground haunts. In this stage of the journey we must make use of the warrior's fierceness, courage, and aggression to break through the rigidities of old structures of manhood and explore the dark and taboo "negative" emotions that make up the shadow of modern manhood.[10]

To go on this kind of inner journey requires certain dynamics if the process is to be successful. Similar dynamics are needed for staying with an experience. Of paramount importance is the willingness to get in touch with one's feelings and to understand the importance of one's emotions. If I am feeling angry, for example, it means staying with the passion to discover its cause and to express the anger appropriately. If I have experienced a significant loss, it involves having the freedom to grieve until such time as healing finally takes place. If I feel sexually attracted to someone other than my wife, it means owning these sentiments, neither repressing them nor acting irresponsibly, working out constructive ways to deal with the situation. If I am in a spiritual dark night, or inner desert, and feel lost and afraid, it requires living in the darkness with patient endurance, trusting that God is somehow present.

Perhaps one of the most difficult aspects of the inner journey is that of becoming acquainted with one's dark side, one's faults and vices. St. Ignatius of Loyola prized this kind of reflection and the importance of self-knowledge because he realized it is at the point of one's weakness that one is most vulnerable to temptation and, thus, regression in the true human journey. In the novitiate, we learned a method to help us discover and fight against anything that would take us away from God called "the Examen." It is more than an examination of *conscience*, it is an examination of *consciousness.* It is a review of what has been happening in us, how the Lord has been working in us, what he has been asking of us, and how we have responded.[11] We will look more closely at this method of reflection in Chapter Eight. For now, it is enough to point out that such an examination takes courage, a courage built on the firm belief of God's unconditional and everlasting love. And it takes faith, the belief that the power of the Holy Spirit to free us from whatever hinders our journey to wholeness (holiness) is greater than our resistances.

Another instrument we will consider more fully in Chapter Eight is the use of a journal as a method for reflecting on one's life. I began keeping a journal in the novitiate. Each evening I would look back over the day in order to see where God was present. Like the Examen, a journal puts us in touch with both our strengths and our weaknesses. Periodically reviewing what we have written helps us to see whether or not we have developed the habit of staying with an experience until it is resolved. If we have not, perhaps this exercise can point us in a direction that will enable this facility to improve.

I realize one can become too introspective. The trick is to get a balance between Socrates' teaching, "The unexamined life is not worth living," and an unhealthy self-absorption. The goals of our reflection are to know ourselves better, to discern how God is active in our lives, to achieve personal integration and wholeness, and to reach out in love to others.

The Jesuit spiritual writer, William Johnston, suggests an intriguing way for staying with a painful experience. He calls it, "the prayer of suffering."[12] He recommends that one simply sit and accept one's cross, accept it totally and unreservedly, be it physical pain, emotional distress, mental anguish, or a spiritual darkness. It is a prayer of silent acceptance. The pain is not a distraction in this kind of prayer, rather it is its substance. One unites one's suffering with that of Jesus on the cross: for the salvation of the world or for particular people. The cross may arise from the ache of loneliness, the torment of betrayal by a friend, an experience of failure, the loss of one's good name, or the fear of dying. Whatever the cause, Johnston writes: "Sit with it. Don't run away. Don't try to escape. Don't fight. Sit with your cross."[13]

Suffering can be creative, as Jesus' passion proves. Buddhism teaches that it is the acceptance of one's pain that leads to peace. Some form of pain is inevitable in life. Peaceful acceptance of it eliminates most of the emotional anguish that can accompany pain—anxiety, anger, fear, grief, impatience, terror. Acceptance of one's pain is also the path to personal growth. Johnston writes:

> Through the prayer of suffering your true self will be born. And this is enlightenment with a vengeance. You throw away your mask; you are knocked off your pedestal; your true character appears; your hidden potential rises up; your personality flowers in a new way; ineffable wisdom comes to possess your being. Above all, you discover a new capacity for love, for a universal love that goes on and on and on. And this is because you have lost your little ego and allowed your true self to be born—the true self that exists in God. And God is love.[14]

Staying with an experience in order to discern its deeper meaning is not solely for the young or those in mid-life. As T.S. Eliot discovered:

> Old men ought to be explorers
> Here and there does not matter
> We must be still and still moving
> Into another intensity
> For a further union, a deeper communion
> Through the dark cold and the empty desolation,
> The wave cry, the wind cry, the vast waters
> Of the petral and the porpoise.
> In my end is my beginning.[15]

Sharing One's Story

Harnan's fourth step to facilitate reflective living is to find someone you trust with whom you can share your feelings and thoughts. This person, or persons, could be your spouse, a male or female friend, your minister or pastor, a mentor, or spiritual director. Whoever it is, the person should be a good listener and able to give you helpful feedback.

As an extrovert, I have found this practice indispensable, as I often get insights about God, myself, and my life in the very act of sharing. For the first fifteen years of Jesuit life, my confidants were fellow Jesuits. Then, I branched out. For the past eight years I have found help sorting through God's invitations to grow and my response with a religious sister who is knowledgeable in the ways of the Holy Spirit. One way I prepare for our meetings is by reviewing what I have written in my journal since our last visit. This helps me to focus my sharing and gives me a clearer picture of what is actually going on in my life.

Not every one is at ease or familiar with opening their heart to another and sharing both the positive and negative aspects of their life. We may need to be taught how to do this by a trusted friend or mentor. Such is the case with Dave. Dave is thirty-eight years old, a project manager for a real estate development company. He has been married for fourteen years. He and his wife, Lucy, have two young daughters. Dave relates how he has learned the importance of being a reflective person.

> Lucy helped me to discover that I have a conscience in my everyday business life. She taught me how to reflect on the past, not to dwell on it, but to learn from it. Sometimes she catches me making wrong judgments about people. Like I would meet someone and be drawn to them for the wrong reasons. She would give me another point of view of the person and I would realize my mistake. My perspective would then change for the better. Sometimes she

asks me how I *feel* about something. My old response was, "What does *that* mean?!" But now I find I stop and consider my feelings: when, for example, somebody annoys me at work, I reflect on what I am feeling and why. I've learned a lot from my wife.

Two keys to Dave's growth in becoming a reflective person are the trust he has in his wife and his humility to recognize truths about himself from another person. He is able to admit his faults to Lucy. Through her love, in both affirming and challenging him, he acknowledges he has become a better husband, father, and worker.

Terry, who is in his mid-forties, is also married and a father. He explains how he came to the realization of the importance of sharing his journey:

> In 1977, I had the wonderful opportunity to make a Marriage Encounter weekend with my wife, Ann.[16] It was a weekend that changed my life in many ways, but probably the most profound change took place in the way I was able to express my feelings with Ann. I used to say, before Marriage Encounter, that I had only four feelings: glad, sad, bad, and had!

> That's all. Those were the only feelings I could identify. Now I can distinguish many feelings and, most importantly, I am not afraid of expressing them with others.

For many men, their closest friend is their wife, as it is for Dave with Lucy, and Terry with Ann. However, this is not the case for all. Some men have related to me on retreats that they are unable to share intimately with their wife either because she is the one not in touch with her feelings or because she is not a good listener. If this is the situation for the reader, you will have to seek someone else who is able to hear what you want to share, who will guard the confidentiality of your sharing, and who can handle this level of intimacy in an appropriate way.

Some men supplement the heart-to-heart encounters they have with their wives with another source. Joe has found additional support in a men's group that developed from a weekend retreat on masculine psychology and spirituality. It has been a locus for the participants to air and share male issues. The gathering is facilitated by a man who is a psychoanalyst by profession. What Joe has learned in these meetings has had positive effects where he works. He explains:

A friend of mine at work had a very tough year because his marriage of twenty years came to a messy end. The effect on him was devastating. At one stage I think he might have been contemplating suicide. He spent a lot of time telling me his story and, thankfully, I was able to use the skills of listening I had learned in our men's group to help him. I even invited him to join the group, which he did, and now it looks like he may have turned a corner.

Tom has also discovered a valuable support system at work. He and his coworkers meet regularly to share on-the-job experiences and problems, finding emotional help especially in times of stress. He says that one result of their mutual sharing is greater productivity.

In summary, then, sharing one's deepest feelings, even one's experience of failure and vulnerability, with a trusted friend or group of friends, promotes the art of reflective living.

Whether you are an introvert, who works things out yourself before discussing them with someone else, or an extrovert, who processes as he speaks, sharing with another can help you clarify and integrate your life experiences. This step, in combination with the other three—slowing down, reconnecting with a deeper order in reality, and staying with an experience in order to discern its deeper meaning—greatly facilitates our journey toward wholeness.

TWO

Male Archetypes and the Shadow

No man should be pitied because every day of his life he faces a hard, stubborn problem. . . . It is the man who has no problems to solve, no hardships to face, who is to be pitied. . . . He has nothing in his life which will strengthen and form his character, nothing to call out his latent powers and deepen and widen his hold on life.

—Booker T. Washington

One of the key instruments I have found helpful to better understand myself and the masculine journey is that of male archetypes. According to authors Robert Moore and Douglas Gillette, there are four basic archetypes of the mature male: King, Warrior, Magician, and Lover.[1]

In the following four chapters, we will consider how these archetypes influence our daily life as men. We will see how they are interconnected: regulating, balancing, and complementing one another.

But here, we'll begin by examining what an archetype is. It was Carl Jung, the Swiss psychologist who died in 1961, who uncovered the existence of archetypes. They are blueprints which exist in every man and woman, primordial images that affect how we think, feel, and react to life's situations. They are "imbedded patterns of thought and behavior laid down in the unconscious of the human psyche through countless years of evolution."[2] Such an image has recurred in a consistent way for so long that it is considered true on a universal scale. Jung believed that the varieties of human experience have somehow been genetically coded and transferred to successive generations.[3] In other words, archetypes are part of our psychic equipment.

Archetypes abide in what Jung called the collective unconscious. Jacob Needleman describes this realm as the ancient, ancestral, psychic life lying beneath the surface of the individual ego. They cannot be experienced directly, but only through means such as dreams and transcendental experiences.[4] Nevertheless, knowing about them, in both their positive and negative characteristics, can give us valuable insight into why we act as we do. Knowing more clearly the false aspects of each archetype, we can learn to alter potentially damaging behavior. And, as we will see in the next four chapters, we can also access more fully the positive traits of each.

It is often in literature and movies that we can discern the existence of archetypes. For example, in the movie, *Dances With Wolves*, there are clear references to the Hero, King, Warrior, Magician, and Lover. The main character in the film, John Dunbar (played by Kevin Costner), ventures out to the furthest reaches of the realm and there takes over an abandoned outpost. In the going, he is acting out the Hero archetype. Once there, he fixes up the unused house and organizes the materials he finds there. He is King of this establishment. He is in his Warrior energy both at the beginning of the movie, as a soldier, and later when he defends the rights of his new friends, the Lakota Sioux tribe. As a way of reflecting on his ongoing experience, he keeps a journal in which he both writes down his thoughts and feelings and draws what he sees. He is in touch with Magician power. Finally, we see him in touch with Lover energy in his friendship with the Indian people and as he falls in love with a woman from the tribe. We will visit this movie again in the following chapters, delving deeper into the significance of the archetypes.

In the United States, and perhaps in other Western countries, the first archetype most men access is the Warrior. The Warrior encompasses competing in sports activities, fighting for a just cause, competition in the work place, and so forth. Ann Brennan explains:

> [This pattern] is operative whenever one sets out with determination to achieve one's personal goal or to free, liberate, or save another or others. The qualities associated with the pattern of the hero are single-mindedness, courage, fortitude, fearlessness, and assertion of will. The hero is involved with personal power and his acts are outstanding, extraordinary, and impressive.[5]

The most difficult for Western man to acquire is the Magician, which involves the practice of reflecting on one's life experiences, interpreting dreams, and utilizing right-brain thinking, that is, the intuitive way of knowing.[6] In mid-life, there are opportunities for growth and integration of those archetypes that are undeveloped or underdeveloped in our psyche.

Interestingly, when I look back over my own life I realize that my experience of growth in the archetypes is different than the general Western male population. By entering the Jesuit Order at the age of twenty-four, I left the world of competition and embarked on a course of studies, and practice, that took me into meditation, frequent reflection on my faults and virtues, the keeping of a spiritual journal, and various writings on the spiritual life. Consequently, what developed early for me was the Magician archetype and later, the Warrior.

I have found it beneficial to consider each of the four basic male archetypes—King, Warrior, Magician, and Lover—in three ways:

1. In relation to myself, how I am living each, in both their positive and negative aspects.

2. In relation to my father, how he lived each.

3. How like or unlike my father I am.

As we shall see in Chapter Seven, I have been progressively healed of psychic wounds from my father. Since no parent is perfect, it is likely that you have also been adversely affected in some way by either father or mother, or perhaps some other significant adult in one's childhood. The effects of archetypal patterns gone awry in inadequate, or possibly even hostile, parents may manifest themselves in our lives as crippling psychological problems.[7]

I hope that by reflecting on the four basic male archetypes, you will come to a greater understanding of yourself: how you are in touch with their positive energy, how you need to grow for further maturity as a man, and how better to access the archetypal power that is available to you.

The Shadow

Before we move to a fuller consideration of the archetypes, it is important to consider briefly another concept of Carl Jung, that of the shadow, for we shall see elements of the shadow in the rest of this book.[8] According to Jung, the unconscious is the source of both our creative and destructive spirit.

The shadow is a psychological concept which refers to the dark, feared, unwanted side of the human personality. Robert Johnson explains:

> Dr. Jung described the shadow elements in a personality as those repressed or unlived sides of a person's total potential. Through lack of attention and development, these unlived and repressed qual-

ities remain archaic or turn dark and threatening. These potentialities for good and evil, though repressed, remain in the unconscious, where they gather energy until finally they begin to erupt arbitrarily into our conscious lives. [9]

As we mature, we try to embody in ourselves a particular image of what kind of person we want to be: hardworking, honest, a good parent, successful, well-liked. The traits we reject are what make up our shadow side. The shadow is that part of myself that wants to do all the things that I do not allow myself to do: lie, steal, cheat, act violently, be promiscuous, act in a cowardly way, be insensitive to others, and so forth. I have a brief look at the shadow when, after having been overcome with anger at someone, I find myself saying, "I really don't know what got into me." What got into me was my shadow, the primitive, uncontrolled, animal part of myself. The shadow is my personal storehouse of all my unconscious desires and emotions that are incompatible with the way I was raised or conflict with acceptable social standards. The narrower and more restrictive the society in which I live, or the religion I practice, the larger my shadow will be.

I have to find some way of living with the dark side of my personality if I am to be at peace with myself. My mental, physical, and spiritual health are at stake in this, not to mention the quality of my relationships with others. One way I have been personally able to do this is by way of a method of prayer I call the Freedom Prayer. It is a prayer that has come out of my own experience. In this form of prayer I deliberately face my faults, my excessive needs, my fears, and my compulsions. I do so in the light of God's unconditional love for me. Some of the unfreedoms I have come into contact have their roots in my childhood.

The prayer is quite simple. Once I have isolated a particular unfreedom or fear (this is the hard part), I bring it to God for healing. I use words such as, "Lord, please free from the excessive need. . . ." And then I name whatever the need may be, for example, to be respected, thanked, praised, in control, successful, preferred to others, etc. Or I may say, "Lord, free me from the fear of failure." Again, I may name some other anxiety such as the fear of change, intimacy, rejection, or the unknown.[10] This prayer has helped me to acknowledge my shadow, to face it, and to become free of its potential disastrous effects on my life.

This process is similar to what Jungians call "befriending" one's shadow. Dr. Diana Greg explains:

> I must first meet my shadow and learn to live with this formidable, and sometimes terrifying, aspect of myself. If I am in search of wholeness and union with God, I must recognize the opposites within me. A person must cherish and cultivate whatever strange, ugly, or beautiful, growths appear within. I must work on this material, describing it, modeling it, striving to bring it into form where it can be contemplated and studied so that its hidden meaning can be discovered. This is the way to inner transformation and wholeness.[11]

By reconciling myself with my darker side I can achieve balance and integration. On the other hand, if I repress the shadow, it acquires strength and becomes even more vigorous so that when the moment arrives that causes it to appear, it is more dangerous than ever, more likely to overwhelm the rest of my personality.

One place we can recognize the shadow is in our dreams. In our dreams the shadow appears as a human figure whom we dislike or react to in a negative way, or who tries to do us harm. I have learned, through practicing dream analysis, to turn towards such threatening figures either by confronting them or by being friendly towards them. Sometimes I am able to do this in the middle of the dream, other times after I wake up and have written down the dream. [12]

Not all that is stored in the shadow is evil. William Miller, in his book, *Make Friends with Your Shadow,* helps to clarify this:

Beyond evil itself we find in the shadow so *much* of personhood that is undeveloped or underdeveloped—diamonds in the rough, so to speak. The shadow contains more than unwanted evil tendencies; there are normal, healthy instincts that have never seen the light of day, realistic insights that may have emerged but were relegated back to the nether region for whatever reason, and creative impulses that may introduce a person to virtually a whole new experience of life.[13]

I encountered an underdeveloped aspect of my personality about six months after my father died. I was fifty-one when Dad passed away. He had a lively sense of humor. However, when he was in his shadow his humor descended to sarcasm. To be the butt of one of his derisions was a painful experience. I have always had what I thought was a good sense of humor, but it wasn't until after he died that I realized I had not fully expressed it because of a fear that I, too, would misuse it. Some form of healing took place in me, and a new wit emerged. I notice this change in me especially when I am giving retreat presentations. Many people have commented how my humor helps to make the more serious and challenging thoughts palatable. I feel a new sense of wholeness as a result of letting go of the fear of misusing my humor and owning, fully, this God-given gift. What had so long remained underdeveloped in my shadow has now surfaced. I, and others, are the better for it. ✝

As we consider the four basic male archetypes, new insights may appear for you, both affirming and challenging. Negative areas of your personality, your shadow, may need to be faced if you are to further advance towards wholeness. Having the courage to acknowledge these will be a necessary tool for the journey, a voyage of redemption and transformation to greater fullness of life.

THREE

The King

A man must go on a quest
to discover the sacred fire
in the sanctuary of his own belly,
to ignite the flame in his heart,
to fuel the blaze in the hearth,
to rekindle his ardor for the earth.

—Sam Keen

We are not used to thinking in royal terminology today. However, lest the reader think that this archetype has disappeared, the father of a family, the president of a corporation, a police chief, the captain of a ship, a pastor or bishop, indeed anyone in a position of authority, needs to access the energy of the King if he is to govern well.

The King energy is primal in all men; it underlies and includes the rest of the archetypes. A wise King is also a good Warrior, a helpful Magician, and a magnificent Lover. The King has the power to create a realm and to provide a sense of security for those in the kingdom, that they might grow and flourish. A good King encourages those in his realm to develop and use their gifts. He does not see this as a threat to his own position.

Soon after I was ordained a priest, I had the pleasure of working for a true King. He was the provincial, or superior, of all the Jesuits in my province (about five hundred at that time). I was assigned to his staff. He has the ability to perceive talents in his subordinates and to draw forth the gifts of their personality and temperament. He and I would meet regularly. I would bring him up to date on what I had accomplished since our previous visit. He would listen, affirm or challenge what I was doing, and then suggest some new avenue for my emerging talents. I blossomed under his leadership.

There are two functions of the King when he is in his fullness. First, he is the one who holds the domain together. He does this with clarity, focus, and purpose. He is the organizer, the vision-maker, the one who codifies laws and makes sure they are just. Here is one man's explanation of how he lives these characteristics of the King energy in his occupation. Dave shares his story:

> I have a talent to organize and enthuse those around me, establishing a vision and setting a pace to realize it. I believe this approach, or perspective, was developed when I was a boy. My parents and siblings encouraged these gifts in me by their praise and respect for the work I did around our house and even at the homes of our neighbors.

To be effective, the good King must embody the spirit of the law in himself. If he does this, his kingdom will flourish. Men like this are found in all walks of life. Terry advises small businesses on how to be more successful. He reflects on his commitment to honesty in the work place:

> I think about ethics all the time in my work. I am very careful to only charge my employer actual miles accrued on my car and never make personal long distance phone calls on his time (I had to fire a guy once for that reason). More importantly, however, in my role as an adviser and educator to business owners, I am oriented to only suggest what is within the law. This may be in areas such as hiring and firing,

keeping accurate and verifiable business records, and reporting correct expenses and revenues to the IRS.

Sometimes embodying the spirit of the law is not immediately appreciated by one's boss. Joe relates his experience:

One of my jobs is responsibility for all the water meters in a particular section of the city. Each week I get an up-to-date print-out of all the customers who have not paid their water bill and thus have to have their service discontinued, that is, have their water turned off. In years gone by, the person in my role would have sent a couple of workmen out to turn the water off and remove the meter without warning. You can imagine the anxiety this caused in our customers. When I got this responsibility, I decided to try a new angle. I phoned the delinquent customer, or went to their home and told them honestly that I was going to have to turn their water off because of their unpaid bill. I explained that this really annoyed me, and asked if there was a way it could be paid. I told them that if it was a case of a shortage of cash that I could arrange for them to pay the outstanding amount in partial-payments, over a six—month period. At first I got a lot of flak from my boss for being "too soft." I argued that the object was to get bills paid, not turn people's water off. He still could not agree with me. Eventually, his boss congratulated me as I was actually saving the Water Department a lot of money due to the savings in workmen's time disconnecting and reconnecting meters. Now my approach is standard practice.

Staying true to one's values in the workplace can be a challenge. It can even be stressful at times. Consider the experience of Dick who worked for over thirty years in the area of human resources:

My work was always satisfying, but dealing with personnel problems became very stressful. It was not always easy to balance Christian principles like love of neighbor and forgiveness with work transgressions like habitual tardiness, absenteeism, or theft. The ethic of giving your best effort for a day's wages was instilled in me by my parents and teachers. Honesty and hard work are the traits I value most highly.

Being a person of integrity continues, of course, beyond full-time employment. Carl, a retired teacher of developmentally disabled children, reflects on his experience:

Now that I am retired, I can do any kind of work I want. Since wages are of secondary importance now, I can also volunteer my time. I tend to do things that put me in contact with people who are less fortunate than I am, for example, the homeless. I try to bring to these situations a sense of honesty and hope, and an open ear to people who need to be heard.

The good King knows his authority within himself. Therefore, he is not threatened by the growth in maturity of those around him. If he is a father, he is not jealous of the giftedness of his son(s). As I related in Chapter One, my father had a definite dark side to his personality. In terms of the King archetype, he was often more tyrannical at home than benevolent. Because he had a low self-image, he sometimes put others down to build himself up. I think his motivation was unconscious for the most part, but the results to the family were hurtful nonetheless. I experienced his putdowns especially when I was in high school and was beginning to come into my own. On the other hand, in certain areas, he affirmed and promoted my gifts. He did this especially in his own area of business expertise. He was a natural-born salesman. As one of his colleagues remarked at the reception following his funeral, "Your father could sell anything to anyone!" He also started his own business. He passed on the gift of salesmanship to me, his eldest child, as well as the ability to be a self-starter. From him I also learned how to be responsible in the use of time and money. Though we were thriving financially, I earned spending money by doing everything from mowing lawns to working in a supermarket. Since Dad was in the food business, he had a special interest in the latter work.

The second function of the King in his fullness is fertility and blessing. Here are Moore and Gillette on fertility in ancient times:

> As the mortal king went, so did the realm, both its order and fertility. If the king was lusty and vigorous sexually, could service his often many wives and concubines and produce many children, the land would be vital. If he stayed healthy and strong physically, and alert and alive mentally, the crops would grow; the cattle would reproduce; the merchants would prosper; and many babies would be born to his people.[1]

The fertile King knows how to create new life in others. He realizes that the kingdom will be the better if others grow. This is the CEO who actively encourages his subordinates to get further education and training. This is the bishop or pastor who believes in collegiality and practices it. None of these feel threatened by the advancement of their subordinates.

The King also has the power to bless and to curse. Blessing can be a psychological or spiritual bestowing. As a Catholic priest, I am very aware of the power of a blessing, and how it can bring peace to someone who is troubled or strength to another for their faith journey. I also know what it is to receive a blessing from an older man, perhaps a mentor, since in the Jesuits I have been blessed by many such men. I have been fortunate to have mentors when I needed them. Such a benediction can have both psychological and spiritual consequences in one's life.

Len is a retired college football coach. He expresses the King blessing in a beautiful way:

As a coach I tried hard to instill in my players a strong work ethic and a desire to work as a team. In dealing with the thousands of young men over the years, I tried to treat each one as I would treat my own son. I feel that any young man who participated in our program had to leave a better person for the experience or else we had failed him.

Many authors on masculine psychology, today, suggest that young men are starving for a blessing from older men, from the King energy. Perhaps it's because of our obsession, in the United States and Europe, with material things, that we have forgotten how to bless our sons with love. Or, perhaps, the need is greater today because of the number of families who do not have a father living at home.

Jesus blessed his disciples with his presence by entrusting to them his teaching, and by his confidence in their ability to preach the good news. In Biblical terms, the true King is described in the Psalms:

A person who obeys God in everything
and always does what is right,
whose words are true and sincere,
and who does not slander others.
He does no wrong to his friends
and does not spread rumors about his neighbors. . . .
He always does what he promises,
no matter how much it may cost (Psalm 15:2-3, 4).

This is the man of integrity and humility, never too proud to ask God for help in order to govern wisely. "Give me the wisdom I need to rule your people with justice and to know the difference between good and evil," King Solomon prayed (1 Kings 3:9). The Psalms also speak of the *compassion* of the true king.

He rescues the poor who call to him,
and those who are needy and neglected.
He has pity on the weak and poor;
he saves the lives of those in need.
He rescues them from oppression and violence;
their lives are precious to him.
Long live the king! (Psalm 72:12–15).

Modern writers on masculine psychology maintain that a man comes to the fullness of the King archetype only after the age of fifty, after mid-life integration. By then, his children are grown, he's reached a certain position in his career, has greater self-knowledge than he had as a young man, and has been tested by some of life's adversities.

Moore and Gillette summarize the characteristics of the true King.

The King archetype in its fullness possesses the qualities of order, of reasonable and rational patterning, of integration and integrity in the masculine psyche. It stabilizes chaotic emotion and out-of-control behaviors. It gives stability and centeredness. It brings calm. … It defends our own sense of inner order, our own integrity of being and of purpose, our own central calmness about who we are, and our essential unassailability and certainty in our masculine identity. It looks upon the world with a firm but kindly eye. It sees others in all their weakness and in all their talent and worth. It honors them and promotes them. It guides and nurtures them toward their own fullness of being. … It rewards and encourages creativity in us and in others.[2]

The False King
Each archetype has both a positive and negative structure. We have considered the former already in this chapter. The negative possibilities in the King archetype are

described in the myth of the Fisher King. This is the wounded father figure. Richard Rohr explains:

> The wound (of the Fisher King) seems to be in the groin. The implication seems to be a wound in sexuality or in fertility. He is not a fertile king. Therefore, the whole kingdom is not fertile. The crops are dying, the monasteries are empty, the people are depressed. All the king can do, because his wound refuses to heal, is fish all day—that is why he is called the Fisher King. . . . All the citizens know that as long as the king is sick, the kingdom is going to be sick.[3]

There are two aspects of the False King: the Tyrant and the Weakling. Unlike the good King, the Tyrant hates, fears, and envies new life because he senses it as a threat to his kingship. He is insecure. In the Bible this is King Herod who ruthlessly had all the baby boys in Bethlehem and the surrounding area massacred because of his fear that one would one day supplant him (See Matthew 2:16-18).

The Tyrant may have a low self-image which could lead him to put down others in order to build up himself. A substantial part of my father's dark side was precisely in this false image of the King. He could be a Tyrant, and without warning. I can recall as a boy being confused at times because he could slip back and forth between being a nice guy and an angry person within seconds. He was so unpredictable. I mentioned earlier in this chapter that he had low self-esteem, but it wasn't until I was far into adulthood that I discovered the reason for his psychological make-up. He grew up with a low opinion of himself because of something traumatic that happened to him as a child. Unfortunately he never had the benefit of counseling so he carried this emotional wound for the whole of his life. In Jungian terms, he never befriended this aspect of his shadow.

One sad consequence of Dad's wound was that I grew up with an inferiority complex, a case of the sins of the father being visited on the son (see Acts of the Apostles 7:51-52 for a Biblical example of this dynamic). Someone has to snap the neurotic chain. In Chapter Seven, I will share how I have been able to break this damaging cycle in our family. I thank God for the true Kings I have known in the Jesuits, for it is through their love and encouragement, and God's grace, that I have come into my own true self, my own true King-ness.

What I have described as happening in our family, which mainly took the form of verbal abuse, could be this and a lot worse when a father is acting out of the Tyrant mode. Moore and Gillette explain:

> It is the Shadow King as Tyrant in the father who makes war on his sons' (and daughters') joy and strength, their abilities and vitality. He fears their freshness, their newness of being, and the life-force surging through them, and he seeks to kill it. He does this with open verbal assaults and deprecation of their interests, hopes, and talents; or he does it, alternately, by ignoring their accomplishments, turning his back on their disappointments, and registering boredom and lack of interest when, for instance, they come home from school and present him with a piece of artwork or a good grade on a test. His attacks may not be limited to verbal or psychological abuse; they may include physical abuse. Spankings may turn into beatings. And there may be sexual assaults as well. The father possessed by the Tyrant may sexually exploit his daughters' or even his sons' weakness and vulnerability. [4]

Having benefited so much from the guidance of older men, I cannot emphasize enough the importance of male mentors, especially in our time when there are so many fatherless families. Boys need more than a mother's care; they need a blessing from men, from good Kings. And young men need help to face their dark side, to come to terms with the Tyrant within, if that is what they have inherited. They need this in order to be good husbands and fathers, to be good bosses and leaders.

Behind the Tyrant resides the Weakling. He is insecure and in his experience of powerlessness he overcompensates by putting so much of his identity in the King archetype that he feels he is nothing unless he can be identified with the King energy. He lacks inner substance. He has a need to be adored, revered, especially by younger men. In fact, he doesn't know how to relate unless he is revered. A biblical example of this false image of the King is Saul. He was so overcome with jealousy at the popularity of his subject, David, that it hindered the effectiveness of his leadership. In 1 Samuel 18:6-9, we read:

> As David was returning after killing Goliath and as the soldiers were coming back home, women from every town in Israel came out to meet King Saul. They were singing joyful songs, dancing, and playing tambourines and lyres. In their celebration the women sang, "Saul has killed thousands, but David tens of thousands." Saul did not like this, and he became very angry. He said, "For David they claim tens of thousands, but only thousands for me. They will be making him king next!" And so he was jealous and suspicious of David from that day on.

Earlier we saw how the good King knows his authority within himself. The Weakling, however, lacking in substance, is also deficient in integrity. He lacks the centeredness, calmness, and security within himself of the good King and this can lead him into feelings of paranoia. He has, in fact, much to fear because his oppressive behavior towards others incurs their dislike and increases the likelihood of their action against him. The story of King Herod, in the New Testament, is a case in point. He thought everyone was out to get him, that even members of his own household were plotting to overthrow him. He had numerous people put to death, even his favorite wife, Mariamme. She was innocent of any plot against him, but he was unable to hear her protestations of guiltlessness. He was caught in the false king, in the Weakling aspect.

Another manifestation of the Weakling is the jealous husband who resents other men paying attention to his wife, who tries to curtail her activities because of his insecurity, or who suspects her of infidelities even though there is no evidence of such behavior. Some men are so insecure they encourage their spouse to get fat so other men will not be tempted to look at them. This is Weakling behavior with a vengeance.

Questions for Reflection

As we seek to access the fullness of the King energy, the following questions are offered as an aid in this process.

1. What leadership qualities does or did your father have?

   In what ways is or was he a good King?

   In what ways, a false King?

   What characteristics of the King archetype did he pass on to you?

   In what ways are you like or unlike your father?

2. In what ways are you a good King?

   In what ways, a false King?

   What characteristics of the good King do you need to access more fully?

3. Who have been or are the significant male mentors in your life?

   How are you a mentor for young men?

   Who needs your blessing?

FOUR

The Warrior

If our cause is a mighty one, and surely peace on earth in these days is the great issue of the day, and if we are opposing the powers of darkness, of nothingness, of destruction, and we are working on the side of light and life, then surely we must use our greatest weapons—the life forces that are in each one of us. To stand on the side of life we must give up our own lives.

—Dorothy Day

The Warrior is a basic building block of masculine psychology and, therefore, also of masculine spirituality.[1] It is a character trait that makes men capable of moral outrage and principled action, but not necessarily physical combat. It includes ardent passion for a just cause and may involve feats of heroism.

The Warrior in his fullness constitutes a total way of life. It is a stance towards life that rouses, energizes, and motivates; it is an aggressive stance.[2] For me, this way of life is captured beautifully in the following prayer of St. Ignatius of Loyola who, before his conversion, was a knight in battle.

Lord Jesus, teach me to be generous,
teach me to serve you as you deserve,
to give and not to count the cost,
to fight and not to heed the wounds,
to toil and not to seek for rest,

to labor and not to seek reward,
except that of knowing that I do your will.

Many women today are uneasy with this form of masculine energy. There are some misuses of it which come from the false Warrior, for example, battering of women and abuse of children. Some opponents would like to curb Warrior energy in men. However, when an archetype is repressed it simply goes underground and emerges in the form of emotional or physical violence. Rather than repressing Warrior energy, it needs to be understood for the positive qualities it possesses and channeled appropriately.

Robert Moore and Douglas Gillette explain how the man accessing the Warrior knows what aggressiveness is appropriate according to the circumstances.

> He knows through clarity of thinking, through discernment. The Warrior is always alert. He is always awake. He is never sleeping through life. He knows how to focus his mind and his body. He is what the samurai called "mindful." He is a "hunter" in the Native American tradition. . . . As a function of his clarity of mind he is a strategist and a tactician. He can evaluate his circumstances accurately and then adapt himself to the "situation on the ground," as we say.[3]

One such modern Warrior is Joe Montana. As a quarterback he had an uncanny ability to adapt himself to the "situation on the ground." He was unparalleled in his clarity of vision on the football field. He was the consummate strategist, especially when his team was behind in the fourth quarter, leading them to thirty-one comeback victories. I have a photograph of him in my office, taken from an article on his retirement from football. His back is to the camera; mud cakes his jersey and his pants. He is standing, looking downfield, ready to call another play.

In carrying out his action, the Warrior has the ability to withstand pain. He is willing to suffer—physically, emotionally, or spiritually—to achieve his goal. This is Jesus on the way to Jerusalem for the final time, doing God's will, even though it meant great suffering. He could say, with the prophet Isaiah, "I have set my face like flint, knowing that I shall not be put to shame" (50:7 NAB).

As I mentioned earlier, shortly after I was ordained a priest, I was appointed Province Director of Social Ministries. This was in 1972. At that time, most Jesuits in my province did not want to hear about social justice. I believe many saw it as a threat to their ongoing work in schools, parishes, and retreat houses. They expected someone in my position to tell them to leave these ministries and get involved directly with people who are economically poor. I, for my part, had a fear of rejection. Yet one of the first activities my provincial asked me to do was to visit the Jesuit communities in the province and speak to them about social justice and the Jesuit vocation. A psychologist friend told me that my fear of rejection had to be faced if I was to be able to carry out the will of the provincial. He explained that this is the fear that we will be unacceptable to someone (or to an organization) that we like, admire, respect, or love. The people that I most admired, respected, and loved were my brother Jesuits. Yet I had also learned about the value of integrity, that if I was true to myself and my beliefs it really didn't matter what others thought of me.

Armed with courage and my firm belief in the value of my integrity, I went from Jesuit community to Jesuit community carrying out the provincial's mandate. I prayed fervently before each presentation. I learned the importance of speaking my truth, but always with compassion for the audience. I received inspiration from these words of the prophet, Isaiah:

> The Lord says,
> "Here is my servant, whom I strengthen—
> the one I have chosen. . . .
> I have filled him with my spirit,
> and he will bring justice to every nation.

He will not shout or raise his voice
or make loud speeches in the streets.
He will not break off a bent reed
nor put out a flickering lamp.
He will bring lasting justice to all.
He will not lose hope or courage (42:1-4).

"Bent reeds" and "flickering lamps" became symbols for me of Jesuits, especially those who were wary of what message I might bring.

As a consequence of my commitment to the virtue of integrity, I was able to act out of the Warrior energy and deliver the message of social justice and Jesuit spirituality. That I did so effectively was largely due to God's power at work in my weakness, the fear of being rejected. Because of this fear, I came across as low-key and non-threatening, as many Jesuits told me. When I first began giving these presentations I used up so much psychic energy just getting up in front of a roomful of Jesuits and delivering the talk that the following day I would be emotionally spent, exhausted! As my confidence grew, I expended less psychic energy.

The Warrior has a commitment beyond himself: to a good king, a just cause, God, a nation, his family, his children. His loyalty is to something of value greater than himself. Lancelot to King Arthur, Martin Luther King, Jr. to desegregation, Cesar Chavez to equal rights for farm workers, Nelson Mandela to a new South Africa, Pope John Paul II to the "culture of life." This is what the Greek philosopher Aristotle called the *summum bonum*, the greatest good. True happiness comes from pursuing the greatest good; to be happy is to be good.[4] The Warrior's questions are: What is the greatest good? What gives my life meaning? What are my values? To whom or to what do I owe my final allegiance? For what or whom am I willing to die?

In everyday modern life, this is Steve who spends much of his free time attending his three daughters' sports events and being daughter Annie's Little League baseball coach. Annie has Down's Syndrome and is on a team that is in the Challenger Division of Little League, a division for children with physical and mental disabilities.

This is Mike whose family owns a car dealership, who cheerfully conveys his Christian faith into his work environment, challenging those around him. As he relates:

> Because of the perception of the car business, I have a golden opportunity to bring my Christian values and ethics into the work place in an effort to make a difference. Honesty and integrity, fairness and loyalty are some of the values I try to live out each day.

This is the teenage boy who dares to be different, who refuses to take drugs and does so by standing up to peer pressure. This is any man, or boy, who is willing to sacrifice immediate gratification for his goals. Robert F. Kennedy said it all so well:

> Few are willing to brave the disapproval of their fellows, the censure of their colleagues, the wrath of their society. Moral courage is a rarer commodity than bravery in battle or great intelligence. Yet it is the one essential vital quality for those who seek to change a world that yields painfully to change.

The true Warrior knows both his strengths and his limitations. He knows when to say yes to a challenge and when to decline. He understands how to harness his reserves—emotional, mental, physical, spiritual—for the long haul. He has stamina for the cause. He is on a journey, which he realizes can be arduous at times, so he has to conserve his energy in order to complete his task.

A few years ago I came across a beautiful story about the Elk and Elk medicine, seen from a Native American perspective. It seems that Elk was in danger, being stalked by Mountain Lion. Elk bolted for the high country when he sensed the presence of his enemy. We pick up the story there:

As Elk made a running leap for the timberline, Mountain Lion gained on him, but Elk continued to run onward, displaying tremendous stamina. Finally Mountain Lion gave up, having spent his energy in spurts as he tried to jump over boulders to reach Elk. Elk paced himself, making headway as he climbed skyward toward the high country. Elk had no other defense except his ability to go the distance, setting a pace that allowed him to utilize his stamina and energy to the fullest.[5]

The Elk is an excellent image for the Warrior. "Elk medicine teaches that pacing yourself will increase your stamina. Elk medicine people may not be the first ones to arrive at a goal, but they always arrive without getting burned out."[6] I am reminded here of my friend, Terry, who is the father of five children, three of whom are teenagers. All five children are still living at home. After dinner, he often heads to bed for an hour's nap before taking on the chore of helping the children with their homework. His wife, Ann, generously takes charge of the family so Terry can get recharged.

The Hero's Journey

In the first chapter, we briefly considered the "Soulful Quest." Sam Keen describes it as a pilgrimage into the depths of the self in order for men to discover their true masculinity. On the way, one must utilize Warrior energy, especially courage and aggression, to face our inner demons and dark shadows. Joseph Campbell defined the Hero as the "man or woman who has battled past his or her own limitations to become fully human."[7] The Hero/Heroine has also been described as one who has lived through pain and been transformed by it. In other words, I have not become bitter or despaired. I have worked through my emotions—fear, grief, anger—and have been able to integrate my suffering, my tragedy. It is vital that one do more than simply endure pain, one must also be transformed, or changed, to have completed the true human journey. With faith, I can discover how God was with me in this negative experience, this physical pain, emotional or mental anguish, this spiritual darkness. However, we should be prepared for the reality that it may be some time before we fully realize how God was present.

In mythology, this journey through pain is seen to have three phases: *Departure, Struggle,* and *Return.* We will consider each phase in theory and how each might relate to our own lives.

Departure

This is the point in which the Hero leaves all that is familiar: you may leave one grade in school and move on to the next, leave family in order to start your own, move to a new city or country, change jobs, or retire. Or, someone may leave you: your children grow up and move out of the house, or a close friend dies. In your spiritual life, God may lead you into an inner desert, to a "place" you have never experienced before. To embark on the journey means to let go of what seems safe and to cross a threshold into unknown territory. Paradoxically, even a bad situation can seem "safe" because we are used to it. Thus, the alcoholic or drug addict has to hit bottom in order to realize he has a problem; someone in an abusive relationship may have to be severely scared before doing something to end it; I might have to hit depression before I realize I need counseling for an emotional problem. The aggressive stance of the Warrior will be needed to move out of a wounded state and to face the situation with courage. Sometimes, this first step on the journey is triggered by a crisis or a sense of having lost control of things: arrested for drunk driving, I realize I have a drinking problem; I discover our child is on drugs and that the whole family needs to be involved in his or her recovery; viruses keep attacking me until I realize I am overworking and need time for rest and play; or my spouse confronts me with an ultimatum, "Spend more time with the family or face a divorce!" In the Departure phase we are challenged to face our fear of the unknown and move toward a seemingly more dangerous but richer zone of consciousness: sobriety, freedom from drugs, a non-abusive relationship. Departure involves risk, choosing a new way of living, letting go of former ways of thinking and acting. One needs trust in God's love and care as a whole new relationship with God begins. Psalm 71 is a good passage to pray in the departure phase, especially the following verses:

> Lord, I have come to you for protection;
> never let me be defeated!
> Because you are righteous, help me and rescue me.
> Listen to me and save me!
> Be my secure shelter
> and a strong fortress to protect me;
> you are my refuge and defense.
> Sovereign Lord, I put my hope in you;
> I have trusted in you since I was young.
> I have relied on you all my life;
> you have protected me since the day I was born.
> I will always praise you (Psalm 71:1-3, 5-6).

Struggle

This is where the Hero descends into the darkness and is transformed. This is Sam Keen's "spelunking in Plato's cave," confronting the dark shadows within that have held us captive in order to be free and own our true masculine gifts. Descending into the darkness can be anything from entering into an alcoholic rehabilitation program or getting counseling because of an abusive personality to facing painful father-wound memories from childhood or being taken by God into a dark night of purification.[8] This transformation cannot happen without the Hero experiencing pain of some kind. During the Struggle phase of the journey, true transformation can only be born out of pain. In religious terms, this is taking up one's cross. I have often found it helpful when I know I am entering into a purifying process to consider the second Station of the Cross where Jesus accepts his cross. I look at him and pray for his disposition, to have his willingness to take on whatever pain is necessary—emotional, mental, physical, spiritual—to go through this next phase of the journey. And then I move on with renewed faith and courage.

A prayer from the Spiritual Exercises of St. Ignatius is appropriate here.[9] It is called, *Anima Christi*, or "The Soul of Christ." The following is a modern translation:

> Jesus, may all that is you flow into me.
> May your body and blood be my food and drink.
> May your passion and death be my strength and life.
> Jesus, with you by my side enough has been given.
> May the shelter I seek be the shadow of your cross.
> Let me not run from the love which you offer,
> But hold me safe from the forces of evil.
> On each of my dyings shed your light and your love.
> Keep calling to me until that day comes,
> When, with your saints, I may praise you forever.
> Amen.

In the Struggle phase the Hero must contend with new and unknown forces that are a challenge. There may be one's own resistance to change or the fear of the pain involved. Other people, even so-called "friends", as poor Job experienced (Job 3-31), or someone who is dependent on us as we are and doesn't want us to change, can try to hinder our growing. In addition, to use a religious concept, there may be an evil spirit who doesn't want us to be transformed except in a negative direction. St. Paul was very aware of the opposing forces within the human heart. In the following passage, he is addressing the Christian community at Ephesus.

> Build up your strength in union with the Lord and by means of his mighty power. Put on all the armor that God gives you, so that you will be able to stand

up against the Devil's evil tricks. So put on God's armor now! Then when the evil day comes, you will be able to resist the enemy's attacks; and after fighting to the end, you will still hold your ground (Ephesians 6:10-13).

This is <u>strong Warrior language</u>. Prayer, of course, is one of the indispensable components of God's armor. We are to pray often, asking for God's help to continue in the struggle. Paul, again using Warrior terminology, exhorts the people:

So stand ready, with truth as a belt around your waist, with righteousness as your breastplate, and as your shoes the readiness to announce the Good News of peace. At all times carry faith as a shield; for with it you will be able to put our all the burning arrows shot by the Evil One. And accept salvation as a helmet, and the word of God as the sword which the Spirit gives you (Ephesians 6:14-17).

During the Struggle phase the Hero is assisted by forces that come to his aid. There is the support of true friends who want what is best for us, and the spiritual strength that comes through the Eucharist and prayer. I often find scripture passages and other prayers from daily Mass to be a source of encouragement. During one extended period of purification, when my patience and tolerance for the battle was running low, I came across this sentence from Psalm 27: "Wait for the Lord with courage; be stouthearted and wait for the Lord" (v. 14, NAB). At other times, something from an article or a book will speak reassurance to my spirit. As I mentioned briefly in Chapter One, shortly after my father died, in 1990, my sisters and brother and I decided to sell the family home. This was very difficult for me since I do not have my own home. Soon afterwards, I found out that a new pastor had decided to renovate the rectory where I had been living for three good years, and that I would have to find a new place to live. Three significant losses in the space of a month! In the midst of my grieving and feeling the insecurity of not having a place to live, I wondered what had happened to God. A short time earlier, a friend had given me a book on the art of surrendering to God. I picked it up during this dark period of my life and read the following sentence:

> We are troubled and disturbed, yet nevertheless in our depths we have some unseen anchor that keeps us clinging to God.[10]

I *knew* in that moment that God was indeed present even though I did not *feel* his presence because I heard God speaking to me in this quote. The "unseen anchor" was my faith, which gave rise to new hope.

The Struggle phase of the journey is the crucible in which the raw untested material is fired. It is a time to pray for courage, for patient endurance, for deeper faith, and for greater trust. A helpful practice when in the struggle is to remember times past when God delivered you from a difficult situation. This memory has the power to strengthen you in the present. Fortunately, the Struggle phase is not the end of the story. There is the Return.

Return

At the end of the journey, the Hero returns at last to where he began, he returns home. His journey is a circle, he returns to the beginning. However, he reappears with a new level of consciousness that those who have not made the journey may not understand. He comes to a new sense of self, to a greater wholeness and inner freedom. This is the alcoholic who has achieved sobriety, the addict who is now drug-free, the workaholic who has learned how to take time off. This is the person who is diagnosed with a terminal illness, who struggles through a myriad of emotions, and comes at last to a peaceful acceptance of his life-threatening condition.

In the celebration of the Return, the hero may not seem different on the outside because the transformation is the result of the inner journey he has made. With his new level of consciousness, the Hero experiences a serenity that is not shaken by any lack of understanding, or doubt, of those around him.

When I reflect on my own life, I find these three phases especially clear in my relationships with women. When I departed for the Jesuit Novitiate, at the age of twenty-four, I was convinced that a necessary part of my commitment was the cessation of friendships with women. This decision came partly from a fear of making a mistake and returning to the promiscuous ways of my past. However, in my desire to follow Jesus completely, I went overboard in my reaction to women and dropped into an emotional dungeon of repressed feelings. The struggle between my fears and God's invitations to be a whole person, a whole priest, that is, one at peace with both men and women as friends, took twenty years! Now I find myself with many women friends, single, married, and religious. I am in the Return phase. I have been transformed. The difference now is that Christ is the center of my life. T.S. Eliot eloquently describes the Return:

> We shall not cease from exploration and the end of
> all our exploring will be to arrive where we started
> and know the place for the first time.[11]

Characteristics of the Warrior

One aspect of the Warrior archetype is just anger. Some examples of Jesus' just anger are his turning over the money changers' tables in the Temple (Mark 11:15-17) or challenging those scribes and Pharisees who exploited the poor by calling them frauds and hypocrites (Matthew 23). Some men have integrated their angry feelings and are able to express them appropriately. Others are swamped by such emotions and lash out in destructive and harmful ways. In my case, I did not learn how to be angry until I was in my mid-twenties. My father wouldn't allow his children to respond to him with anger. Consequently, I, for one, repressed it. When I finally came to the realization of this, I sought counseling. In the therapeutic process I learned how to let angry feelings surface and how to express them appropriately. As I was able to do this more and more, the day finally arrived when I could confront my father. He was surprised. I was elated. From that day forward we began to be friends. In later times we had our differences, but now we could argue them out. We sometimes lost our tempers in the process, but never to the point of severing the friendship. Becoming a true Warrior took a significant leap forward for me through this experience.

Real Warriors have the humility to learn from their mistakes. Not to do so is to be doomed into repeating them. I remember hearing an impassioned declaration of this truth from a gang leader. He believes that only gang members can prevent gang violence in the community. "You only learn from your mistakes," he said. "Instead of grabbing our guns, we have to be the ones to stop the violence for the kids."

Learning from one's mistakes is especially important in marriage. A few years ago I met a man who was into his third marriage. Unfortunately he still hadn't learned this important lesson. His attitude was, "The past is past; I don't think about it; I just move on." Move on he does, continuing to disappoint and hurt those in his family. In contrast to this person, consider the following reflections by Dave, who is in his late thirties: "I believe that a closer walk with Christ has helped me to become the man, husband, and father that I am. Not perfect! But accepting and acceptable. A man able to admit fault and error."

A man living out of the Warrior archetype has a positive outlook on life. Neither the trials of life nor the calamities in modern society have the power to grind him down. Dick has been retired for five years. He relates this about his life:

With all the troubles in the world, my family and I have been able to find peace and tranquility. A guiding principle for me has always been a saying my mother displayed on our kitchen wall. It stated: "I felt sorry for myself because I had no shoes and then I saw a person with no feet." I think everything in life is good, it is just that some things are a whole lot better than other things—so I stay focused on the good things.

Mario's positive perspective especially affects his work. Here is his experience in his own words: "Work is what I do best and therefore succeed in doing. I consider my work a wonderful form of recreation and pleasure." Work is so enjoyable for him that sometimes he likens it to an adventure. In Warrior language, he articulates his vision:

Whether it be work or play, the motivation for both stems from the need to win. Winning is the reason to continually pursue the endeavor. It is striving for the "trophy" that is the reward and ultimate recognition, that keeps me coming back to the repetitiveness of a task.

The Warrior enables us to go on despite what the body says. This demands discipline. It takes sacrifice to stick to a diet, to exercise regularly. One has to concentrate to stay abreast of developments in one's profession, to learn a new task, to stay true to making time for prayer in one's life. It takes discipline to do what you have to even when you don't feel like doing it. And it takes patient endurance.

The Warrior is always in search of a good king, someone whose cause is just, someone to whom he can give his wholehearted commitment. In the Spiritual Exercises of St. Ignatius, one of the most inspiring meditations is called "Christ the King and His Call." After reflecting on how appealing it is to follow an inspiring human leader, Ignatius has the retreatant consider Jesus Christ and his invitation to

"Come, follow me." Jesus' call goes out to the whole world, yet he calls each person in a unique way, according to each's personality and talents. He makes this appeal: "It is my will to win over the whole world, to conquer sin, hatred, and death—all the enemies between humanity and God. Whoever wishes to join me in this mission must be willing to labor with me, so that by following me in suffering, he may follow me in glory."

Ignatius then proposes that persons who are of great heart, who have a great love for Jesus, will not only offer themselves completely for such a mission but will act against anything that would make their response less than total. They would want to make a commitment like the one captured in these words:

> Eternal Lord and King of all creation, humbly I come before you. Knowing the support of Mary, your mother, and all the saints, I am moved by your grace to offer myself to you and to your work. I deeply desire to be with you in accepting all wrongs and all abuse and all poverty, both actual and spiritual—and I deliberately choose this, if it is for your greater service and praise. If you, my Lord and King, would so call and choose me, then take and receive me into such a way of life.

I made the Spiritual Exercises of Ignatius in its thirty-day form ten days after entering the Jesuit novitiate. This meditation on the call of Christ the King had a profound effect on me, energizing the spiritual Warrior energy within me as I had, at last, found a King worthy of living and dying for. Warrior energy must be connected to the other male archetypes—King, Magician, and Lover—or the results will be devastating. This is so because the Warrior in his pure form is emotionally distant. His focus is on his cause. It is a transpersonal loyalty which radically relativizes the importance of his human relationships.[12] His devotion to duty can render him oblivious to those around him, even his family, if, for example, his profession demands long hours of work. Even dedication to a religious goal can fall into this trap. I recall an instance from my own life that bears this out. I had been living in Berkeley, California for about five years when a possible ministry opening came up on the east coast. I considered the request and told the inquiring Jesuit that, subject to my provincial's approval, I would be interested. Later, I shared all of this with a close nun friend. In the midst of my excitement about this great possibility, she wanted to know why I hadn't mentioned this to her when the job opportunity first came up. "After all," she said, "we are good friends; don't you think I have a right to some input about a ministry opportunity that would take you far away from me?" To be honest, I had never thought of doing this with her. I figured, if God wants me to move east, I'll go! My friend's response caught me up short and helped me to realize that single-minded devotion, even to God, has to take into consideration other people's feelings. I learned through this experience that the Warrior needs Lover energy in order to keep him relating with other persons in a compassionate and loving way as he follows his call.

The False Warrior

Pat Arnold, in his thought-provoking book, *Wildmen, Warriors, and Kings*, points out that those who would be Warriors are charged with certain sacred obligations: never to act violently out of blind anger or revenge, and to take full responsibility for their actions.[13] This brings us to a consideration of the abuse of these two responsibilities.

There are two manifestations of the False Warrior: The Sadist and the Masochist.

The Sadist can emerge when the Warrior is too detached from human relationships. Then Warrior energy is twisted and becomes cruelty. The image that comes to mind is the actor, Jack Palance, in the movie, *Shane*. He plays a gunfighter, hired by some cattlemen to terrorize farmers in order to frighten them into leaving their land. He personifies the False Warrior as he takes advantage of the vulnerability of the farmers. He acts without compassion and is devoid of love for people.

The Warrior run amuck can be seen in the horrific bombing of the federal building in Oklahoma City in 1995. This is anger out of control. What the Warrior needs above all is a conscience. He needs to know right from wrong according to society's standards. He needs a code of ethics. Recall the knight's code of King Arthur's Round Table: personal honor, noble restraint, magnanimity to defeated rivals, and humility for one's deeds.[14] He requires a disciplined mind and feelings that are under control. Otherwise, the Sadist will win out. Richard Rohr states it this way: "A Warrior is always dangerous if he is not in submission to a (good) King. When the Warrior loses contact with the wisdom of the King to tell him which battles are worth fighting and which are not, he is in trouble."[15]

When we are severely frightened or when our anger is out of control, destructiveness is not far behind. Anti-government militants, terrorists, Ku Klux Klan, neo-Nazi groups are fearful, angry people. Psychologist Michael Cavanagh describes how fear and anger are often intimately related.

> Most angry feelings rebound off feelings of fright. Most "hostile" people are frightened people; most "arrogant" people are frightened; most "snobbish" people are frightened. When we can understand this, it opens up a new dimension of relating to ourselves and to others. If when I'm angry, I can ask myself "Underneath my anger, what part of me is frightened by what just happened?" and "What just occurred that threatened my self-concept?" I will have more data with which to understand myself and to communicate this fear to the source of the threat. . . . This is not to say that all anger can be traced to fear, but a good deal of it can.[16]

The Sadist is lacking in compassion for those who are weak and vulnerable. If he has a family, his behavior can degenerate into child abuse or wife-beating; if he is in law enforcement, to police brutality; if in the military, to atrocities. If he is in a position of authority, he will put down his subordinates and treat them unjustly.

The second manifestation of the False Warrior is the Masochist. In this negative form, a man feels powerless. He allows others to dictate his life for him. He doesn't stand up for his own needs and desires, which means his inner boundaries are not protected. The true Warrior protects his boundaries, but the False Warrior doesn't know how to say no. He lets his wife or his children, his boss or his work run him. He is insecure. He is lacking in the aggressive stance toward life of the true Warrior.

The Masochist needs to recapture the masculine determination of the Warrior, that posture toward life that energizes us, that pushes us to take the offensive. When I find myself feeling powerless over some major task facing me, I like to watch the movie, *Chariots of Fire*. The courage and resolve of those men, on fire for the glory of the Olympics, lights a flame within my own spirit and inspires me to action. St. Paul exhorts us in times like these: "Lift up your tired hands, then, and strengthen your trembling knees! Keep walking on straight paths, so that the lame foot may not be disabled, but instead be healed" (Hebrews 12:12 -13).

The man in bondage to the Masochist needs to find balance in his life. If he allows others or his work to dominate him, he will lose his self-respect, as well as his mental and physical health. He may need a crisis to bring him to his senses. The following story is a good example.

> Andrew, a Navy vet who became director of staffing at a large consulting firm, faced himself down one day. He was spending some two hundred days per year on the road, logging hundreds of thousands of miles away from his wife and their four children.

Despite the stress and personal privation, he recalls, "It felt good to be doing well in my job. The adrenaline rush of success is a narcotic." That year he returned from a business trip a week before Christmas and woke up the next morning seized by massive chest pain. He spent the next several days in the hospital, recovering from a coronary incident. Flat on his back, listening to the judgmental metronome of a heart monitor, he did some serious thinking. "Why does the price of success include giving up family life, when your family is the reason you're working so hard?" The enforced contemplation led Andrew to drastically reengineer his life.[17]

Questions for Reflection

As we seek to access the fullness of the Warrior energy, the following questions are offered as an aid in this process.

1. What positive characteristics of the Warrior do you see in yourself? Here are some examples: aggressive alertness, a passion for justice, integrity, just anger, a willingness to suffer to achieve your goals, compassion for the weak, compassion for yourself, the humility to learn from your mistakes, a positive outlook on life, discipline, respect for women. Add your own.

   What positive characteristics of the Warrior does or did your father have?

   Who have been the "good Kings" in your life? The just causes?

2. In which phase of the Hero's journey are you now— departure, struggle, or return? What characteristics of the Warrior do you need to access in order to successfully complete this phase? What do you need to let go of in order to move on to the next one? You can use this technique to

consider the whole of your life journey or a particular time in your life.

3. What aspects of the False Warrior do you find in yourself? Here are a few possibilities: unintegrated anger, cruelty, settling disputes by resorting to violence (in word or deed), lack of compassion for the weak and the vulnerable, inability to say no, letting others run your life (or your work). Add your own.

   Does or did your father have any aspects of the False Warrior? How did these manifest themselves?

   What energizes you when you are feeling powerless?

4. Who are some positive male Warrior models for you, living or dead? Men you have known, read about, seen in movies or watched in sports? What do you admire about them? How can you more fully access these traits for yourself?

   The next time you feel really angry about something, stop and ask yourself, "Underneath my anger, what part of me is frightened by what just happened? What just occurred that threatened my self-concept?"

FIVE

The Magician

The Way that I have been shown by my grandparents and your grandparents is the way of love and respect. It is the way of patient watching, listening, hope. It is a way of generosity and humor that tries to keep all things in a balance. It is a way of acceptance and surrender to our Common Origin, our Common Ground, our Common Home.

—Patrick J. Twohy, S.J.,
Chaplain to the Swinomish Native Americans

The Magician archetype expresses the world of sages and shamans, of faith-healers and confessors, of medicine men and yogis, of hermits and those who can discern spirits, of ministers and priests.

A shaman, according to the dictionary, is a person who acts as intermediary between the natural and supernatural worlds, using magic to cure illness, foretell the future, and control spiritual forces. The shaman restores wholeness and fullness to both individuals and the community.[1] It is that part of us that seeks fullness of being, that desires, in mythologist Joseph Campbell's words, "to feel the rapture of being alive."

As we will see in this chapter, Magician energy has many faces. The Magician energy is the wellspring of awareness and insight, of inner wisdom, of conversion and transformation. We connect with it when we analyze our dreams by trying to make sense of the symbols delivered to the conscious self by the unconscious. We discover it on the right side of the brain, home to our intuition. It is the source of the art of reflective living, and we need its energy to discern between good and evil, between good spirits and bad spirits. It stimulates the Hero in us to make our journey from Departure, through Struggle, and to Return. But it is also from the Magician that the wily Trickster originates, popping our balloons of self-importance and vanity with his timely messages of reality.

The Magician is the master of technology, the keeper of secret and hidden knowledge of all kinds.[2] Thus, inventors and scientists, astronomers and mythologists, doctors and lawyers, technicians and mechanics, therapists and computer analysts, priests and preachers all draw from the Magician's well. In this archetype lies the origins of our psychological, scientific, and technological discoveries. Albert Einstein, Jonas Salk, Joseph Campbell, Carl Jung, Henry Ford, Bill Gates—each had the gift to see into the depth of things and each became an initiator of others. We see the same dynamic at work in gifted coaches like John Wooden, "The Wizard of Westwood," or Bill Walsh, the genius of the San Francisco 49ers. The true Magician is the one who has the interests of people and of the planet in mind, and who shares his accomplishments with others in a compassionate way.

Robert Bly, Sam Keen, and Richard Rohr are three leaders of the men's movement who have tapped the Magician's energy. They have each gone into their own souls to discover what it is to be a mature man. Through retreats and workshops they seek to bring other men to a deeper appreciation of the positive characteristics of masculinity. By means of poetry and story, metaphors and myths, they point the way past male sins of machismo and repression of the anima. The *anima* is the name that Carl Jung used for the feminine aspect of a man's personality. Subjugation of the anima leads to the oppression of women, persecution of homosexuals, and exploitation of the earth. Magicians guide men by their example to a greater integration of the animus and the anima, of the rational and the intuitive, of commitment and courage.

On June 4, 1995 Bill McCartney, former head football coach at the University of Colorado, attracted 42,900 men to the Promise Keepers gathering at the Houston Astrodome. McCartney started the organization in 1990 to help men to be more godly, to honor their commitments to family, and to grow into greater maturity. He came to this insight through his own conversion. Reportedly he heard a preacher say a man's character will be reflected in his wife's countenance, but looking at his wife, he saw pain. He asked for and received her forgiveness for chasing his own dreams at the expense of hers.

Promise Keepers is founded on seven key promises:

1. A Promise Keeper is committed to honor Jesus Christ through worship, prayer and obedience to his word, in the power of the Holy Spirit.

2. A Promise Keeper is committed to pursue vital relationships with a few other men, understanding that he needs brothers to help him keep his promises.

3. A Promise Keeper is committed to practice spiritual, moral, ethical, and sexual purity.

4. A Promise Keeper is committed to build strong marriages and families through love, protection and biblical values.

5. A Promise Keeper is committed to support the mission of his church by honoring and praying for his pastor and by actively giving his time and resources.

6. A Promise Keeper is committed to reach beyond any racial and denominational barriers to demonstrate the power of biblical unity.

7. A Promise Keeper is committed to influence his world, being obedient to the Great Commandment (Mark 12:30-31) and the Great Commission (Matthew 28: 19-20).[3]

McCartney is tapping into something profound in men. He is seeking integration of the archetypes of King, Warrior, Magician, and Lover through the seven promises. A true Magician, he points others in the direction toward real fulfillment. He invites men to access the Magician's energy to create balance in their lives, to integrate the masculine and feminine. Notice, Promise Keepers is not built on dominating one's wife, but on working with her in a partnership of love to foster a healthy marriage and family life.

The guidance of the Magician is a strong theme in the movies. In *City Slickers,* Curly (played by Jack Palance) takes the role of the Magician when he tells the middle-age would-be cowboy that there is just one thing necessary for happiness. It is up to each man to find it and then be true to it. Obe Wan Kanobe, the wise man of the *Star Wars* trilogy, guides Luke Skywalker to an appropriation of the mysterious "force" by which evil can be fought and overcome.

In *Dances with Wolves,* Kicking Bird, the Indian holy man who befriends John Dunbar, helps him to learn the cultural ways and language of the tribe such as the dance around the fire, the importance and ethics of the buffalo hunt, and other important traits of his people. He also aids and encourages John in his quest to become a "true human being," much as a modern-day father would counsel his son. John, for his part, accesses Magician energy when he makes friends with the wolf, a symbol of the wildness of nature. He touches the power of the Magician as he dances around the fire in front of his own dwelling, celebrating his experience of the buffalo hunt. And he keeps in contact with his inner Magician by keeping a journal, reflecting in word and artistic sketches on his experiences.

The Magician has the gift to see into the depth of things. Sigmund Freud discovered the realm of the personal unconscious. Carl Jung took humanity a step further with the discovery of the collective unconscious, the abode of the archetypes, those "building blocks of our thoughts and feelings and of our habitual patterns of behavior and reactions."[4] Paleontologist Teilhard de Chardin expanded the phenomenon of consciousness to include all that exists. In his "Law of Complexity-Consciousness" he postulates that there is no such thing as brute matter. Everything has some germ of inwardness. He wrote:

> Everyone has known from the beginning that organized matter is endowed with spontaneity in combination with psychic inwardness. Everyone also knows today that this organic matter is amazingly complicated. . . . Absolutely inert and totally brute matter *does not exist*. Every element of the universe contains, at least to an infinitesimal degree, some germ of inwardness and spontaneity, that is to say of consciousness.[5]

The Magician is in touch with nature. St. Francis of Assisi, who had a genuine and deep respect for the integrity of creation, understood the intimate connection between God and all creatures. We are all dependent on God for the very air we breathe. Francis inspires us to have a sense of joy and wonder as we contemplate a beautiful sunset or fish in a quiet stream, as we hike in the mountains or stroll by the sea. For Francis, every living thing is a mirror of God's presence and, if approached with respect, a step leading one to God.[6] In this way, nature can become a departure point for reflection.

Not too long ago, I discovered how powerful a force nature can be in helping men become more reflective. In the early 1990s I gave a two-day workshop on masculine psychology and spirituality to twenty men in Belfast, Northern Ireland. I was a bit nervous going into this weekend because of the civil unrest in Northern Ireland. In addition, I had heard stories of how difficult it is for Irish men to share their feelings. This workshop was designed to help the men remember and face, in a healing way, memories of how they might have been wounded as children, either by their father or mother. We were also to consider the four basic male archetypes and how they affect our lives. The men ranged in age from their mid-thirties to mid-sixties and they came from a variety of backgrounds. From the beginning of the workshop, I found them open, willing to get in touch with past hurts and even to share their experiences with one another.

On the afternoon of the second day, we considered the effect of Magician energy in their lives. I asked them to take a leisurely stroll in the neighborhood, to be alert to natural things, to trees and flowers, to the sounds of birds, to the movement of squirrels and other creatures. I encouraged them not to analyze what they saw, but simply to *be* with it.[7] If some object "found them," that is, spoke symbolically to them about themselves, about life, about God, they could bring it to Mass (if, indeed, it was transportable!) as an offering to God. I was amazed as these men, inundated by twenty-five years of violence in their country, brought a leaf, a twig, a stone, a flower, a blade of grass, and spoke from the heart of the significance of each for them.

The Magician is the archetype of awareness and insight. Wilferd Peterson writes of this facility for reflection in his book, *The Art of Living:*

> The art of awareness is the art of learning how to awaken to the eternal miracle of life with its limitless possibilities.
>
> It is searching for beauty everywhere, in a flower, a mountain, a machine, a sonnet and a symphony.
>
> It is developing the deep sensitivity through which we may suffer and know tragedy . . . but through which we will also experience the grandeur of human life.

It is identifying yourself with the hopes, dreams, fears and longings of others. It is learning to interpret their thoughts, feelings, and moods.

It is keeping mentally alert to all that goes on around you; it is being curious, observant, imaginative that you may build an ever increasing fund of knowledge of the universe.

It is striving to stretch the range of eye and ear, it is taking time to look and listen and comprehend.

It is through a growing awareness that you stock and enrich your memory, and as a great philosopher has said: "A man thinks with his memory."[8]

There is power in Magician energy to be used for the good of people and the planet. The true Magician is the one who shares his knowledge of technology in a compassionate manner. Whatever your profession—car mechanic or electrician, teacher or shopkeeper, firefighter or policeman, computer programmer or politician—are you using your expertise for the good of others as well as your way of making a living? Not over-charging for your services and making others feel stupid when they are not as knowledgeable as you are positive examples of Magician energy. Whom does your knowledge serve? What are your talents for? If only for money and prestige, then the false Magician is at work in you.

A couple of years ago I had one of those annoying experiences where the cure threatened to be more expensive than the problem. An audio cassette got chewed up in my tape deck and I couldn't get the little window open. Fearing the worst, I took the whole contraption to a nearby radio shop. The technician took a quick look at the problem, said, "Aha!", went to his tool box and came back with a regular kitchen knife in his hand. Deftly he slid the knife behind the tape and out popped the window that had the tape trapped. He unraveled the spool of what now was a useless tape and offered his condolences. When I asked how much this little operation would cost, he smiled and said: "Oh, nothing. I'm just glad to be of help." That's compassionate application!

The Magician knows how to use his gifts prudently. If one is an initiator of some psychological or spiritual insight, compassionate dedication emerges in the following manner. The initiator always has to have in mind the capacity of the receiver to receive, to be able to integrate this new knowledge in a wholesome, healthy way. In other words, the other person's (or group's) ego strength is important. I remember reading about a conversation between Thomas Merton and Phil Berrigan regarding the Vietnam War. Both men were opposed to the war and Berrigan was making the point that to continue to be a person of integrity he would have to proclaim the truth. To which Merton responded: "Truth is important, but we have to be careful with truth. It can slice someone in half if they are not ready to hear it or if we present it in such a way that it damages their dignity rather than enhances it."[9]

Overloading another's psyche is dangerous. My friend, Joe, has worked this out in relation to his children. He explains:

> As my children grow older I feel I should tell them more and more of my personal story to date, but only what I feel each can comfortably handle. What I share with my ten-year-old son Aidan is different from what I share with Ciara, his twenty-year-old sister. I think it's important for their own journey to know my stuff because they are part of me in a very real way.

Richard Rohr explains this important aspect of the Magician archetype:

> I am aware of my personal sinfulness, yet I cannot deny that I wear the mantle of the magician. I am being used somehow for the transformation of people. It would be a sin for me to deny that; it would be

some kind of false humility. If you have the gift, you have to use it. Each man has his mantle, which he has to learn to wear with grace and dignity. That's masculine energy—to carry out what he has been given to do. To do otherwise would be unfaithfulness to the Lord. . . . To think it is *you* would also be unfaithful.[10]

The Inner Journey

The Magician is the archetype of inner work, of the Hero's journey. I draw from Magician power when I set out on a journey to find my true self. My true self is the person beyond the false, incomplete, superficial self.[11] St. Paul wrote about this in his letter to the Ephesians:

> Get rid of your old self, which made you live as you used to—the old self that was being destroyed by its deceitful desires. Your hearts and minds must be made completely new, and you must put on the new self, which is created in God's likeness and reveals itself in the true life that is upright and holy (Ephesians 4:22–24).

Thomas Merton proposed the model of the true self and the false self to help us understand ourselves and to show us the way to peace and happiness. He understood that this was also the means by which we would discover the person of God within. He wrote:

> The secret of my identity is hidden in the love and mercy of God. . . . Ultimately the only way I can be myself is to become identified with God in whom is hidden the reason and fulfillment of my existence. . . . Therefore there is only one problem on which all my existence, my peace and my happiness depend: to discover myself in discovering God. If I find God I will find myself and if I find my true self I will find God.[12]

There are various aspects of the false self. In our society, the false self often emerges when we invest our identity and self-worth in externals: what we own, where we live, what others think of us. It is identity by comparison rather than identity by uniqueness. In religious terms, it is serving an idol instead of the real me. And, although it may lead to temporary fulfillment, it is not a recipe for true happiness.[13]

To discover my true self, my false self must die. This is a life-long journey, but there are many rewards along the way. Moments of wholeness, of being at peace deep down even when turmoil rages in one's life; a sense of meaning; healing of past hurts; a greater capacity to give and receive love from others: all are experiences of the true self. There is one thing necessary: commitment for the journey.

Native Americans called this journey the Vision Quest. The following is a description of how a boy entered into his first Vision Quest.

> For a youth, the time of the first Vision Quest took place when puberty was beginning and he began to assume the stature of a man. To become a hunter and a warrior, he needed a guardian spirit. But to find this spirit, it was necessary to fast. The body, depleted through lack of food, became receptive to the spirits within the world of nature, spirits that appear in visions during dreamlike trances. When a boy or his father believed the time was ripe, the youth was offered either food or charcoal at breakfast. If he chose charcoal, he rubbed it on his face as a sign that he would seek his guardian spirit. Then father and son left their wigwam and sought a likely place in the woods to build a rude shelter that would house the boy for as long as four days of almost total fasting. The shelter completed, the father returned alone to the village while the boy began his quest. As hunger sapped his vitality, the boy sat and waited, falling into a fitful sleep from time to time, until in

his deep reverie, the ardently sought guardian spirit came to him. The youth might dream of this spirit several times before he was certain that he had truly found his personal guide and protector. In some instances the spirit would confer unusual endowments—creative powers or the gift of prophecy—upon the youth. But in any case, the spirit that came during a boy's initial vision quest remained with him for life. Direct contact between spirit and warrior would periodically be renewed via additional vision quests.[14]

With the exception of some Native American tribes, we do not have such an intense rite of passage for boys in the United States. Some kind of ritual is important to alert a boy to the significance of passages in his life, of the need for an inner guide on the journey, and of the value of reflecting on one's experiences in order to learn from them.

We might be tempted to think that having a guardian spirit is old-fashioned and out-of-date. Not so according to a national opinion poll taken in the winter of 1995. It showed that over 70% of Americans believe in the existence of angels. This is obvious from the number of greeting cards and paintings people are buying with the images of angels on them. We even have a postage stamp with an angel on it!

Whether one believes in spirits or not, each of us needs guidance and support if he is to descend into the depths of himself, if he is to cross the void between the false self and the true self. In the Old Testament, the Psalmist directs our attention to the Good Shepherd:

He gives me new strength.
He guides me in the right paths, as he has promised.
Even if I go through the deepest darkness,
I will not be afraid, Lord, for you are with me.
Your shepherd's rod and staff protect me
(Psalm 23:3-4).

Traveling inward also takes trust in God's healing grace. Pat Arnold explains the dynamic of this spiritual reality.

> Grace is God's unexpected and gratuitous help that, to uninitiated and unaware people, seems like blind luck or good fortune, but to Magicians it is the secret force that unfolds our lives in love and wisdom. Grace is God's magic that heals our diseases, reconciles our friends, turns around our defeats, and washes away our sins; grace is that "extra" force that ought, by rights, *not* be there for us, but is—if only we will accept it.[15]

Native Americans see the Raven as the bringer of Magician power, for in their mythology, it is the messenger of the void. "Raven magic is a powerful medicine," write Jamie Sams and David Carson, "that can give you the courage to enter the darkness of the void, which is the home of all that is not yet in form."[16] They continue: "Raven's color is the color of the void—the black hole in space that holds all the energy of the creative source. In Native (American) teachings the color black means many things, but it does not mean evil. Black can mean the seeking of answers, the void, or the road of the spiritual or non-physical."[17] The Raven is connected to the dynamic of healing: "Raven guides the magic of healing and the change in consciousness that will bring about a new reality."[18] In this view, Raven is the messenger of transformation toward greater wholeness.

Consider the following four accounts of men who have gotten in touch with the Magician on their inner journey. Perhaps what these men relate will help you do the same.

> MYSTERY—*Who Am I?*
> Created by the Unknown
> in mystery. . . .
>
> I am mystery. . . .
> My body and spirit

Both real. . . .
Yet at times
Seeming to exist
In myth. . . .

My unreal self
Exudes pride. . . .
Self stature . . .
Empty desires. . . .

My real self
Swims in emptiness

Sometimes touching earth . . .
And the path . . .

Sometimes experiencing
Mystery . . .
Spirit . . .
Heart . . .
Bits of truth. . . .

Knowing truth . . .
My desire
To share . . .
Dawns.[19]

Give me a candle of the Spirit, O God, as I go down into the deep of my own being.

Show me the hidden things.

Take me down to the spring of my life, and tell me my nature and my name.

Give me freedom to grow so that I may become my true self—the fulfillment of the seed which You planted in me at my making.[20]

My life has led me to a place where I have endured much emotional hardship—a life of pain. But, rather than remaining embittered and resentful I have chosen to "embrace my shadow," and cultivate a resurrective spirit of gratitude. Recognizing that the `shadow' side of me does exist was a pivotal experience. This was by no means an easy task, and by no means is the task completed. It has come after years of confrontive deliberation and implicit trust in my higher power. For embracing does not mean denying or hiding, it does mean validating and accepting. This initial action was imperative in the formation of my spirituality. The death-to-life philosophy I have formulated is based upon how I view death. It has come in light of my own mortality in relation to my loved ones (his brother has AIDS). My prayerful reflection on the Passion of Christ is also reflected in how I perceive death. Death is simply another part of the life process. It is not something to be feared, but embraced. It is easy for me to say this now. For I know that I will dearly mourn someday.[21]

. . . And so, for the first time in my life perhaps (although I am supposed to meditate every day!), I took the lamp and, leaving the zone of everyday occupations and relationships where everything seems clear, I went down into my inmost self, to the deep abyss whence I feel dimly that my power of action emanates. But as I moved further and further away from the conventional certainties by which social life is superficially illuminated, I became aware that I was losing contact with myself. At each step of the descent a new person was disclosed within me of whose name I was no longer sure, and who no longer obeyed me. And when I had to stop my exploration because the path faded from beneath my steps, I found a bottomless at my feet, and out of it came—arising I know not from where—the current which I dare to call *my* life.[22]

Magician energy is at work in these stories. As we seek healing and wholeness, as we uncover unconscious motives and hurtful memories that trap us into negative behavior—sometimes unwittingly repeating the "sins of our father"—as we strive to rid ourselves of the idols of our identity that have accumulated, we come more and more upon our true self, the free self God created us to be.

At the beginning of the book we considered four suggestions from Nicholas Harnan to promote the art of reflective living. The first two are particularly appropriate for accessing Magician power:

Slow down, cultivate a slower rhythm in your daily life.

Reconnect with a deeper order in reality, an order beyond your immediate control.

Oftentimes other men, men we love and trust, help us to reflect on our lives, on both the troubles and the joys. Dave shares his experience.

Over the past six years I have participated in several men's groups, praying and sharing our daily lives and struggles. With one particular group we met once a week consistently for over three years. This was a great experience as I took the opportunity to look back on my week, not to focus on my failings so much but to find the times where Christ was working in my life and me for him. Now that is positive reinforcement!

It is helpful to ritualize in order to make concrete the inner healing that has occurred. In the first day of the two-day men's workshop in Belfast so many emotions came up as the men got in touch with painful childhood memories that I knew we could not begin the second day with a theoretical talk. Instead, we began the day with the following ritual.

I held a lighted candle and suggested that those who wished, when the candle was passed to them, could either be silent for a moment or say either, "I forgive my father (mother) for . . ." or, if the man was not yet ready to forgive, "I *want* to forgive my father (mother) for. . . ." It was a profound moment of awareness and healing for each person, including me as I discovered I was not yet ready to forgive my father for something he had done.

You may wish to celebrate a moment of transformation as well. One possible exercise is to take Psalm 139 and dwell on such verses as:

> Truly you have formed my inmost being;
> you knit me in my mother's womb.
> I give you thanks that I am fearfully, wonderfully made;
> wonderful are your works (139:13-14, NAB).

Another positive exercise is to write your own magnificat, a prayer of praise to God, celebrating God's presence in your life and your own generous response. See Luke 1:46–55 for Mary's prayer, or design your own personal way of celebrating this new advancement toward wholeness as a man.

The Trickster

Lest we take ourselves too seriously in our quest for the true self, the Magician shows us another face, the Trickster. He is "the source of all the irreverent, hilarious, and comic things men do."[23] Dave Barry has captured the essence of the Trickster in his hilarious book, *Dave Barry's Complete Guide to Guys*. The book is dedicated to whoever invented the remote control! Barry expounds on such timely topics as: why guys (a species of men) prefer to believe that there is no such thing as a "prostate," why the average guy can remember who won the 1960 World Series but not necessarily the names of all his children, how testosterone was declared a controlled substance like heroin, and some of the difficulties guys have in communicating their intimate feelings—"assuming they have any." To illustrate the communication problem, he offers the following example.

This is an aspect of guyhood that is very frustrating to women. A guy will be reading the newspaper, and the phone will ring; he'll answer it, listen for ten minutes, hang up, and resume reading. Finally his wife will say: "Who was that?"

And he'll say: "Phil Wonkerman's mom." (Phil is an old friend they haven't heard from in seventeen years.)

And the wife will say, "Well?"

And the guy will say, "Well what?"

And the wife will say, "What did she *say*?"

And the guy will say, "She said Phil is fine," making it clear by his tone of voice that, although he does not wish to be rude, he is trying to read the newspaper, and he happens to be right in the middle of an important panel of *Calvin and Hobbes*. But the wife, ignoring this, will say, "That's *all* she said?"

And she will not let up. She will continue to ask district-attorney-style questions, forcing the guy to recount the conversation until she's satisfied that she has the entire story, which is that Phil just got out of prison after serving a sentence for a murder he committed when he became a drug addict because of the guilt he felt when his wife died in a freak submarine accident while Phil was having an affair . . . but now he's all straightened out and has a good job as a trapeze artist and is almost through the surgical part of his sex change and recently became happily engaged to marry a prominent member of the Grateful Dead, so in other words he is fine, which is *exactly* what the guy told her in the first place, but is that enough? No. She wants to hear *every single detail*.[24]

I wish my father were still alive; he would have loved this book. When I was still a kid, he introduced me to the joy of listening to Bob and Ray on the radio. Dad loved to make puns, and he was good at it. By the time I got to high school I was reading H. Allen Smith's books, like *Life in a Putty Knife Factory* and *The Horse Latitudes*. After Dad died, I went in search of these books to keep as mementos. Reading them again after all these years still tickles my funny bone.

Tricksters come in a wide variety of shapes and sizes, as jesters and clowns, comedians and mimics, punsters and satirists, even practical jokers. Whether your taste runs to Bill Cosby telling us what happened when he took his three-year-old daughter to the football game or Tim Allen wise-cracking about life in the TV show *Home Improvement*, comedians help us to laugh at our own foibles. Emerson said it well: "The perception of the Comic is a tie of sympathy with others, a pledge of sanity. We must learn by laughter as well as by tears and terror."[25]

The cartoon, *Doonesbury*, keeps national politics from getting carried away by self-adulation. Monty Python keeps reminding us of the silly things in life, especially in its skit, "And now for something completely different." Hawkeye Pierce and BJ Honeycut kept the MASH unit (and us viewers) from going crazy at the sight of so much suffering. Oldtimers, such as Doodles Weaver and Groucho Marx had the Trickster's gift for irreverence finely tuned. Movies directed by Mel Brooks—who can forget some of those scenes in *Blazing Saddles!*—and Woody Allen's classic, *Bananas*, reveal the absurdities just beneath the reality of life.

In Native American mythology of the West, the Trickster is represented by the coyote, who is seen as a cultural hero.

He is known for his sly, bawdy, capricious behavior. Writes Ake Hultkrantz: "The coyote is a merrymaker who stimulates feelings of relief and malicious joy in his audience because of his many deviances from the norms of social behavior. He acts even during sacred ceremonies to ease the pressure brought on by the tense and solemn atmosphere."[26]

When the Trickster is operating in someone, watch out, nothing is sacred. Consider the following story: A newly ordained Roman Catholic priest was nervously celebrating his first Mass. It is customary to ask a few "veteran" priests to assist the newly ordained and so the young man asked a couple of his friends to do so. Things were progressing smoothly; even the sermon had gone well much to his relief. After preparing the hosts and wine, during what is known as the Offertory, the young priest walked to the end of the altar where one of the assisting priests stood. He was holding a glass bowl filled with water, for it is part of the ritual that the priest dip his fingers into the water as a symbol of purifying them. The newly ordained looked into the bowl and gasped, for there swimming in the water was a goldfish!

The Trickster serves many purposes. The inner Trickster helps to neutralize our pomposity, dogmatism, prejudice, or self-righteousness when we fall prey to these faults. It assists us to see through denial and rationalization. It keeps us in touch with reality, especially when it forces us to face our fallibility. It keeps us aware that we are just as human as everyone else and like every person we too have an "Achilles heel"—that part of our personality that is sorely vulnerable—so that we will be less likely to fall victim to it.[27] The Trickster puts things together where paradox or contradiction reign. It helps us to laugh at ourselves when we take ourselves too seriously.

The ability to laugh at oneself is a precious gift. Once, when I was making my annual eight-day retreat, my retreat director thought I was taking myself too seriously. I was probably trying to be perfect instead of human. She suggested I practice smiling (or at least a half-smile) every time

I made a mistake. After much practice, I finally got the hang of it.

In my retreat talks, I often share funny things that have happened to me. Many people have told me that these accounts lighten a somber mood. My favorite story concerns one Saturday night when I was returning from a full day's work at the parish in Tijuana, Mexico. Saturday is the busiest night of the week to cross the border so I knew I would have at least an hour's wait in the car. I was tired from the day's activities as well as from the work of the previous week. When I am tired, I get testy. Patience is not one of my strong suits anyway. As I sat in the car and inched it slowly forward towards the border, it seemed that everyone in the city was trying to sell me something, or wash the car windows, dust the car, or whatever. Each time someone approached me, they got a more irritable, "No Gracias."

The "straw" that broke my patience came in the form of a Mexican Indian woman who was carrying a wooden rack of stuffed birds, each on a string. She was about ten feet from my car when I spotted her. I leaned out of the window and rudely shouted, "*No Gracias!*" She completely ignored me, came right up to the car, leaned her head towards mine, and said, "Padre?" It was a woman I knew! Out of a city of over a million people, my fall from grace came from Señora Duran, whose family I knew and in whose home I had even shared a meal. "Señora, how are you?" I said, completely mortified. She responded in a friendly way and walked alongside the car as the cars in front of me moved closer to the border crossing, bringing me up to date on her family. After about five minutes, as she was ready to go on her way, I pointed at the stuffed birds she was selling, and asked, "How much?" "Only a dollar, Padre," she responded smiling. "Give me one, please," I said. I hung it over the rear view window to remind me that I can always go one more step in being patient. The Trickster had struck!

Children are especially good at bringing the presence of the Trickster to us. They have a way of bursting the bubble of self-importance when we least expect (but so desperately need) it.

Remember, the Trickster can pop up anywhere. I was in the midst of writing this chapter of the book when I received Dave Barry's book on guys as a birthday gift! Joseph Campbell once remarked, on experiencing the occasional whimsical behavior of his computer, "there's a hierarchy of angels on slats in the Hard Drive!"[28]

The False Magician

Just as the other two archetypes we have considered, King and Warrior, have their dark side, so does the Magician. It is wise to be aware of the potential to misuse Magician power and to guard against it.

We saw earlier in this chapter that the Magician is the master of some sort of knowledge that takes special training to acquire. We also observed that each man has his mantle that he needs to learn to wear with compassion and dignity. Consider the following hypothetical situation as an example of the reverse of this:

You are the manager of a small business. There are many tasks to be done and, although money is not in short supply, you do not want to spend it needlessly. One of your staff realizes she has taken on too many responsibilities and wants to change her status from full-time to part-time. She comes to see you to explain that her family needs more of her time. She has small children and they need her presence at this important period of their lives. She suggests that someone be hired to take some of the load off of her. Although you know that what she says is true, you also know—consciously or unconsciously—that she has a difficult time saying no, especially to someone in a position of authority. You are happy with things as they are. You do not want to be bothered finding another staff person and going through a period of training. Besides, she is a hard worker.

So you manipulate her co-dependent nature, her need for recognition of her gifts, and her inability to stand her ground with an authority figure, in an effort to convince her that everything is just fine as it is.[29] Whether you are doing this consciously or not, this is a gross misuse of the Magician's power. Not only is your conduct a defilement of the archetype, but it is a violation of the basic trust between you, as a manager, and one of your employees. Taking advantage of another's weakness to further one's own goals is cruel and manipulative, the exact opposite of one of the Magician's main values: compassionate application of one's gift.

Or consider the dynamics of an election campaign. People who seek to win by playing on the fears of the electorate, making scapegoats of women on welfare or undocumented immigrants as the causes of present economic woes, or who pit one race against another in order to gain leverage, are acting out of the false Magician. They are misrepresenting the facts and distorting the truth in order to deceive and by this means to win. The irony is that they harm themselves and their souls by their lust for power.

The false Magician is in us when we take advantage of a shortage of supply for something we sell by raising the price, or the rent, to such an extent that the new price puts an unfair burden on those who are economically poor or who are on fixed incomes.

We saw in this chapter that the Magician has a respect for nature. It does not take much analysis to see the false Magician at work against the earth: air and water pollution, clear-cutting of forests, the use of harmful pesticides, strip-mining, underground nuclear bomb testing. The list goes on. The late Bede Griffiths, an English Benedictine priest and spiritual leader who spent thirty-eight years living in India in a Christian *ashram* (a monastery), understood these threats to creation as the result of a fundamental defect in Western society. In his book, *The Marriage of East and West*, he submitted that Western Civilization is out of balance and has been since the Renaissance. He wrote:

The balance can only be restored when a meeting takes place between East and West. This meeting must take place at the deepest level of the human consciousness. It is an encounter ultimately between the two fundamental dimensions of human nature: the male and the female—the masculine, rational, active, dominating power of the mind, and the feminine, intuitive, passive and receptive power. Of course, these two dimensions exist in every human being and in every people and race. But for the past two thousand years . . . the masculine, rational mind has gradually come to dominate Western Europe and has now spread its influence all over the world.[30]

Griffiths suggests that this imbalance is one cause of the domination of man over woman, the white races with their dominant reason over the tribal peoples with their intuitive feeling and imagination, and of human exploitation of the earth. In other words, it is the power of the false Magician. The antidote, he maintains, is for the Western person (which, of course, applies to women as well as men) to seek the integration of reason and intuition, animus and anima, masculine and feminine. We will consider the value of intuition more fully in the next section.

The false Magician is active in the man who does not want to know himself. He buries himself in overwork, alcohol, drugs, noise, or endless mindless activity. He is the couch potato, the computer nerd. He does not want to go on the inner journey. He does not want to learn from his mistakes. He is living a superficial life and prefers to stay that way. Perhaps he is afraid of what he may find in himself. He may think that getting in touch with his feelings is woman's work or for men who are soft. Or, he may realize that inner work can be difficult and he is afraid of the pain he may have to undergo to come to his true self.

We find a symbol for this possible false part of ourselves in Matthew's gospel (25:14-18), in the parable of the coins. Jesus tells the story of a man who went on a long journey. He left his possessions in the care of his servants. To one he gave five coins, to another two, and to the third, one. While he was away, the first two servants invested the money and made more, but the third servant dug a hole in the ground and buried the money. When the owner returned, he settled accounts with the three servants. Pleased with the industriousness of the servants who increased their amounts, he gave them a reward. The servant who buried the coin said: "Sir, I know you are a hard man; you reap harvests where you did not plant, and you gather crops where you did not scatter seed. I was afraid, so I went off and hid your money in the ground" (vs. 24–25). To which the owner responded: "You bad and lazy servant! You knew, did you, that I reap harvests where I did not plant, and gather crops where I did not scatter seed? Well, then, you should have deposited my money in the bank, and I would have received it all back with interest when I returned" (vs. 26–27). Just so, we are not to bury our head in the sand of our ignorance about ourselves, but are to find ways to realize our true selves more fully through the inner journey.

A final example of the false Magician concerns humor. We saw that the Trickster uses humor to help us keep in touch with reality. However, humor can also be used as a weapon. If it is used against people in sarcasm or derision, or in such a way that it puts people down, it is coming out of the dark side of this archetype. In this case, instead of lightening someone's load, they feel worse about life.

The Fullness of the Magician

As we seek to access the Magician, we need to keep in mind how it relates to the other three basic male archetypes. As Moore and Gillette point out: "we need to mix with the Magician the King's concern for generativity and generosity, the Warrior's ability to act decisively and with courage, and the Lover's deep and convinced connectedness to all things."[31] If we do this, we will be living in a mature masculine way.

It is constructive, as we conclude this chapter, to consider some of the practical ways Magician energy manifests itself in our lives. We drew from the experience of others when we reflected on the inner journey and when we looked at the role of the Trickster. It is time now to pull together our reflections.

We draw from the power of the Magician when we seek to make correct life decisions. Steve shares his experience:

In 1989 I began to pray fervently that God would open a door for me somehow, or enlighten me, if it was a time for a career change. The problem was I still enjoyed being an electrician, but I could not face another year of financial setback. During this time I sought counseling and tried to consider every avenue open to me. One night, while I was anxiously pouring through the book, *What Color Is Your Parachute?* (a book on selecting career possibilities), I cried out to God: "What do I do? You know me and you know the desire of my heart and the gifts you have given to me. . . . All I desire is to continue in this line of work and be able to make a fair wage." At that moment I felt an amazing peace come over me and I seemed to hear God telling me to set all my worries aside, that he was taking care of my needs and that I needed to wait patiently. Within a few months I was selected from among forty-nine applicants for a position as electrician within the city's unified school district. Five years have passed since then, and they have been the happiest of my work life."

God speaks to us in many ways. If we can be open to the voice within, we are able to hear the mysterious utterances of our God, pointing us in the direction of inner peace.

Instinct is connected with the Magician. My father was a natural-born salesman. He knew instinctively how to present a product in an appealing way to his customers. He passed this gift on to me. I especially notice it when I am preparing to give a retreat. I meet so many different people, in a variety of cities and countries. Yet I know instinctively how to adapt the retreat material according to my audience.

We see instinct at work in some sports events. I think of Michael Jordan when he gets into his "zone"and cannot seem to miss a shot. Watching Tiger Woods at the 1997 Masters was an absolute delight. The masterful way he managed the course spoke not only of a talent not seen in a person of his age since Jack Nicklaus entered the golf scene, but also of his intelligence, his patience, his discipline, and his poise. We see instinct at work in a marathon tennis match when the players, oblivious to the crowd, volley back and forth with such intensity that we realize they are in a world of their own. It happens to us, too, when in a fast-paced pick-up game of basketball we instinctively know who to pass the ball to. It can even happen at the horse races when, by instinct, we know which horse will be the winner. We are connecting to what scientists call right-brain thinking, the intuitive hemisphere of the brain. Intuition is real knowledge. It allows us to draw on the vast storehouse of unconscious knowledge that includes everything we have experienced or learned, either consciously or at a subliminal level, and the infinite reservoir of the collective unconscious.[32] When we allow this half of our brain to develop, we will experience its salutary effects in both our personal and professional lives. We will be accessing the fullness of the Magician energy.

Questions for Reflection

As we seek to access the fullness of the Magician's energy, the following questions are offered as an aid in this process.

1. Am I using my talents, my expertise, for the benefit of others as well as my way of making a living? For example, do

I avoid over-charging for my services or making others feel stupid when they are not as knowledgeable as I am?

Whom does my knowledge serve?

What are my talents for?

2. Do I value intuition as a real form of knowledge, as equally important for both men and women?

3. How do I feel about the value of inner work, of the inner journey? What qualities, graces, do I need to continue this process?

4. In what ways has the Trickster been operative in my life, within me and in my experience with others?

5. In what ways am I living out true Magician energy? In what ways am I falling short? In other words, how well am I "wearing the mantle of the Magician"?

SIX

The Lover

The day will come when, after harnessing space, the tides, and gravitation, we shall harness for God the energies of love. And, on that day, for the second time in the history of the world, we shall have discovered fire.

—Teilhard de Chardin[1]

Psychologists tell us that there are, basically, three kinds of love: eros, agape, and amor. These three forms of love are included in the Lover archetype.

Eros was the ancient Greek god of love, later symbolized by the Romans as Cupid. Eros encompasses physical love, sexual desire, and sexual attraction. It includes what we experience as "falling in love," or romantic love.

Agape, quite simply, is the love of God for humankind. It is most profoundly expressed for Christians by Jesus Christ's death on the cross. Agape is the brotherly or sisterly love of one Christian for another, corresponding to the model of God's love for human beings. It is the unselfish, self-giving, compassionate love of one person for another, This is the love of the Hero who gives his life to something bigger than himself. Agape is also the quality of friendship known today as male bonding, or brotherly love.

Amor is the complete union of one body and soul with another body and soul.[2] It describes the emotional, physical, and spiritual bonding between a man and a woman.

Amor involves mutuality and is friendship at a deep and profound level.

All three of these loves can be active in a given relationship, although usually one predominates over the others. Followers of Carl Jung often refer to the Latin term *libido* to describe the Lover. While Sigmund Freud saw libido as connected solely with sexual energy, Carl Jung understood it in a more extensive way, as *a general passion for life*. In this latter sense, the Lover is one who appreciates the good things of life, who delights in play, whose senses are alive to the beauty in art, music, and poetry. He is able to feel with others in their pain as well as their joy. This is the man in touch with his own sexuality without shame, the husband who has the sensitivity and discipline to be as concerned about fulfilling his wife's sexual desires as his own, the father who is not afraid to show affection for his children, even if it makes him appear vulnerable at times.

Moore and Gillette sum up this archetype:

> We believe that the Lover, by whatever name, is the primal energy pattern of what we would call vividness, aliveness, and passion. It lives through the great primal hungers of our species for sex, food, well-being, reproduction, creative adaptation to life's hardships, and ultimately a sense of meaning, without which human beings cannot go on with their lives. The Lover's drive is to satisfy those hungers.[3]

A man accessing Lover energy feels connected with all creation. With respect to people, he knows in his heart the truth of St. Paul's insight that when one suffers, all suffer; when one rejoices, all rejoice (1 Corinthians 12:26). He feels in tune with nature. This sympathy with the outdoors leads him to a concern for the integrity of creation, to the conviction that it not be exploited, that it be honored and cherished for it is also a part of him.

Lover energy is what enables us to be sensitive to all that exists outside ourselves, to changes in color, smell, sound, shape, texture, and taste. A simple way to stimulate this kind of awareness is to *pause* at any time of the day and *listen* to everything around you, *look* at everything around you, and *feel* the sensations of your body. This will ground you in the here and now.

The Lover knows himself as lovable and as loved. He has the capacity and the freedom to receive love at a deep, intimate place in his heart. This acceptance takes a lifetime to fully realize, but the Lover is willing to undergo the necessary conversion that will bring about the fullness of self-realization.

Drawing from the Source of all love, his primary conversion is to the belief that God loves him unconditionally, and that this love is personal.[4]

Father Pedro Arrupe captured the intimacy of our spiritual life in this poignant way:

Nothing is more practical than finding God,
that is, than falling in love
in a quite absolute, final way.

What you are in love with,
what seizes your imagination
will affect everything.

It will decide what will get you
out of bed in the morning,
what you will do
with your evenings,
how you spend your weekends,
what you read,
who you know,
what breaks your heart,
and what amazes you with joy
and gratitude.

Fall in love,
stay in love,
and it will decide everything.

Intimacy and the Lover Archetype

Intimacy is an important aspect of Lover energy. According to psychoanalyst Erik Erikson, intimacy is the flexible ego strength necessary for being close to another. That other may be one's spouse, a close male or female friend, one's children, one's parents, or, of course, God. I may have the emotional strength to develop a closeness with each of these others in my life or with only a few. Since intimacy involves self-disclosure, the sharing of one's secrets, and the exposure of one's feelings, I may have just enough energy for one or two intimate friends. This kind of open communication with another human being demands taking risks, the risk of being misunderstood or even of being rejected. It takes courage to face the risks inherent in the sharing of oneself on more than a surface level. Kathleen Fischer and Thomas Hart list four reasons why we shy away from the kind of heart-to-heart sharing that constitutes genuine interpersonal intimacy:

1. *When I open my heart, I make myself vulnerable.* What I say can be misunderstood, used against me, or lightly dismissed. It can be found ridiculous, bad, or boring. And once it's out, it's out; I cannot call it back and restore it to its hiding place.

2. *If I get too close, I will be swallowed up.* I will lose myself, being taken over by you. I will no longer know who I am. I will no longer have a life of my own. If I tell you I love you, you've got me. You will lay all kinds of expectations on me, and I will have no freedom left.

3. *I will be shattered if I lose what I love.* Far safer not to love anyone or anything too much, for loss is total devastation. Those of us who as children lost a parent through death or

divorce know this devastation. Anyone who has formed a close bond of love later in life and then been rejected knows how shattering that is. Once having had such an experience we often vow unconsciously that we will never let ourselves get that close again.

4. *I have never experienced intimacy, and I simply don't know how to get close.* Some people want closeness, but are at a loss how to proceed. Others were so deeply hurt by parental rejection that they move through life with a sort of distant numbness, neither contemplating nor aspiring to intimacy.[5]

I can relate to numbers two and three of these resistances. When I entered the Jesuit novitiate at the age of twenty-four, I reflected on my past relationships with women and was filled with guilt over my sexual activity. I vowed never to have another woman as a close friend. Unfortunately, in my zeal to be perfect I went overboard and ended up repressing my normal, healthy feelings for women. So strong was my fear, and I realize now, self-doubt, that it was ten years before I was freed by God's grace to have a friendship with a woman.[6]

Over the next thirteen years God led me toward greater inner affective freedom by placing in my life a number of wonderful women. Since fear and self-doubt (the concern that I would end up back where I started, sexually) still claimed a corner of my heart, progress was characterized by "two steps forward, one back." Eleven years ago I made a giant leap forward. I became friends with a woman who has challenged me to grow in my capacity to give and receive love. I thought my heart couldn't expand any further in this life, but as a male friend of mine told me, "every time you think you have a grasp on something, God moves the goal posts and it's a whole new ball game!"

As in any close friendship, there have been moments of joy for my woman friend and me, and experiences of pain. One of the key breakthroughs for me was when I realized I was holding back in being open to her because I was afraid

God would take her away from me as my mother had been taken from me. My mother was my best friend. She died when I was twenty years old. When this insight came to me on a retreat, it was a revelation. I brought my concerns to God and asked God to free me from all my fear. I was freed and proceeded to open up to my woman friend in a deeper level of friendship.

A couple of years later I hit another wall in my heart. It came with the realization that my woman friend loved me more than any other woman had since my mother. Over the years I had worked through my fear of losing my vocation by having women as friends. Thus I was surprised at this new level of protest within me to accepting my friend's love. Upon reflection, there seemed to be two parts to this new resistance. On some unconscious level, I had a fear of being over-whelmed by her love. However, there was something else.

A Jesuit friend who knows my history all the way back to childhood, especially my relationship with my father and the rejection I sometimes received from him, suggested that on some level I did not consider myself worthy of my woman friend's love. I prayed over this thought and asked God for a root healing of whatever in me was unable to receive my friend's love fully and freely. God heard my plea because within a short time I found myself able to love her and be loved by her at a completely new level. As in past experiences of transformation, this new capacity for love affected all my relationships. Not only was I able to relate to my woman friend at a deeper level of intimacy, but I discovered an ability to share and relate more deeply with all my friends.

One of the wonders of love in my life is that since I entered the Jesuit order I have come to believe in God's unconditional and everlasting love for me. This love has deepened over the years as I have followed to the best of my ability the graces I have been offered along the way. My realization of God's personal love has transformed my self-image, from a lack of self-esteem to knowing myself as valued and lovable. God's love has also freed me to be more open to receive love from people and to love them in return more fully.

I have grown in quantum leaps in my capacity to love and be loved since those early experiences of conversion in the novitiate. Correspondingly, the level of intimacy with God in my prayer and with both male and female friends has deepened. I credit certain individuals and groups for their assistance in my humanization process: fellow Jesuits, African-American and Mexican people in whose communities I have had the privilege of working, children whose spontaneous affection has helped me to become more spontaneous, women friends who have helped me to become more comfortable and without fear in my sexuality, male friends outside the Jesuits such as the various men quoted in this book, and retreatants with whom I often share what I have learned from my life experiences in order to help them better understand theirs.

Perhaps your work also provides opportunities for sharing your experiences. Here is one man's perspective:

> I bring a lot of my personality and my beliefs into the work place (he works for a public utilities company). Over the years quite a number of my fellow workers have shared deeply with me. Especially the men. They obviously feel safe with me. It could be because I tend to share and talk about real things in my life while a lot of the talk in the canteen is superficial.

Or, take the case of Dave, who works for a development company. He participates in an unusual sharing group at his office.

> There exists a strange form of prayer at my office, at least I call it prayer. It is an opportunity for my colleagues and me to reflect together on our current frustrations and our past experiences in order to conduct a check to make sure we are on solid moral ground in our business practices. We also discuss

our family situations, laughing at times and often tearing over the joys and heartaches we have.

This is intimacy on a group level, but it is nonetheless meaningful and significant for the participants.

Intimacy is the opposite of loneliness. Though we do not like feeling lonely, we know there are enemies to intimacy both within and outside ourselves. Besides the fear of disclosing personal feelings with another, some people are either not in touch with their feelings or uncomfortable with the ones they do acknowledge. In addition, sharing intimately implies trust, trust in the other to honor one's feelings and thoughts. If trust has been betrayed, it will be difficult to let it resurface. One can apply the Freedom Prayer, which I described in Chapter Two, to a variety of fears, specifically in this case, to the fear of rejection.[7]

Some of us grew up in families where intimacy was in short supply. In some cases one parent lacked the necessary ingredients for an intimate relationship; in other cases it was both parents. We learn a lot from our family background. Sometimes it stunts our emotional growth. But it can also be a stimulus for us to act in a different, more healthy way. John shares some of the joys and pains he has encountered with those he loves:

> Intimacy is very important in my life, but only with a select few, my wife Eileen being at the top of the list. I can talk to her about everything. On a physical level, my timing is not always right or I can misjudge the kind of intimacy she is seeking at a particular time. Sometimes she just wants to be held, but being the typical male I misread this signal so that what began as intimate ends up in conflict and confusion. Intimacy with my parents is mixed. I can talk and share with my father on anything whereas with my mother we tend to "box" around each other not letting the other really know what is going on. My mother and I have decided to have a good, long chat

with a third party, a priest friend, as a facilitator. Hopefully this will improve the level of our communication.

Earl relates that he has a distant relationship with his parents in large part because his mother dislikes and is antagonistic toward his wife. He has, however, a very close friendship with his wife. He says:

Rosemary is truly a blessing and we are deeply in love with each other. Our personalities are complimentary as well as synergistic. She has been a guiding light for me along the path to a closer relationship with God.

Gene also has a deep friendship with his wife. She is his closest friend, the one to whom he can and does confide everything.

My wife and I have been through many tough times together and have been able to support and encourage each other. The type of relationship we have in regard to sharing feelings is very satisfactory for me. However, I have a mixed relationship with my parents. My mom and I have a very close level of intimacy. There is probably nothing I can't share with her. The two of us have always been able to talk about any issue in my life. My relationship with my father, unfortunately, is just the opposite. The problem is I cannot get to any level of intimacy with him because he shies away or refuses to enter into deeper discussion. Most of our conversations stay on a philosophical level.

Some of my male married friends tell me their struggle for greater intimacy takes place mainly with their children. Dick, who is both a father and a grandfather, shares his story.

I experience difficulty fully sharing my feelings with my children and now my grandchildren. This comes,

I think, from a fear of being weak and vulnerable with individuals with whom I think I should be an authority figure.

In a similar vein, Steve relates,

Much as I would like to, I find it difficult to share my feelings with my children. Or perhaps I should say with my oldest daughter who is thirteen. I've thought about this a lot and it seems I am too hung up with the father-daughter relationship instead of being a friend. Apparently I am too established in the role of trying to teach, lead, etc. I lack the intimacy that I would like to have with her. I try and work at it, but I have a difficult time letting my guard down. I am affectionate with her as I am with my other two children as far as hugging, but I do not have the comfort of being able to share myself and my inadequacies anywhere near as much as I do with my wife.

Intimacy in marriage demands quality time with your spouse. When there are children in the home, this will mean getting away occasionally, just the two of you, perhaps an evening each week to talk about the past seven days and the things that are important for each of you. Two of the enemies of intimacy are boredom in a relationship and taking the other person for granted. One will need to access Lover energy to seek ways to keep the excitement alive. My friend Gary and his wife Bobbie, whose three sons are grown and out of the house, get away for a weekend on a regular basis, away from the demands and stress of work in order to nourish their relationship. So effective has this practice been that even after thirty-six years of marriage, Gary can say:

My relationship with my wife feels very intimate. I am free to tell her how I feel about anything. Being in love with Bobbie is a spiritual experience. I connect with her all the time, consciously and unconsciously.

The intimacy of our bodies is not only sexual. We seem to be on the same path trying to keep our bodies healthy.

Finally, mutuality in sharing is essential to the kind of communication implicit in an intimate relationship. Though each may share in a different way, depending on whether one is an introvert or an extrovert, mutual self-disclosure has to happen if it is to be a friendship. Otherwise it is counseling. More talkative persons need to discipline themselves to listen with full attention, hearing the words that are being said by their partner and the feelings behind those words. Shy people need to go against their natural inclination to mainly listen and speak up. My friend Maurile points out some of the challenges young married couples face as they seek to communicate openly with one another.

> On top of the demands in ordinary communication, add differences in family background, whether the two people have good self images or poor ones, emotional baggage from the past, quality of intimacy between each one's parents, possible social, cultural, and religious differences, and the expectations each brings to marriage.

No wonder it is said that people *grow* into loving one another! The goal of intimacy is a true quest. It takes courage and patience to achieve. Inasmuch as a man does so, he is drawing from the energy of the Lover archetype.

A Passion for Life

The Lover is deeply sensual. He is sensually aware and sensitive to the outer environment in all its nuances and splendor. He has the patience to stop and smell the roses. He has the discipline to quiet his mind and listen to the sounds around him. Here is some of what we hear when we quiet our minds and listen:

> A bird welcoming the morning,
> ocean waves crashing on the shore,

the hooting of an owl,
the sound of the wind as it brushes a field of hay,
the creaking of a tree limb loaded with snow,
the silence of a desert night,

the cheerful voices of his children,
the sound of his wife's breathing,
laughter, singing, sighing, crying.

This is music that stirs the heart.

Sounds of the factory too,
men shouting, machines clanking,
conveyer belts moving, assembly lines operating,
and the welcome shrill of the 5 o'clock whistle.

Sounds at the office,
phones ringing, printers printing,
a dentist's drill drilling,
coffee break chattering,
and the joyful, "Well done!" to one's latest project.

Wherever the sweat of our brow takes us . . .
students inquiring, athletes encouraging,
sirens wailing, tractors thundering,
and the haunting call of a train whistle in the night

All things are connected for the man accessing the Lover. He values the intuitive and is open to its promptings.

One afternoon I was sitting on a hillside with a friend of mine. We were sharing our spiritual journeys with one another. Before us lay a beautiful valley and other hills beyond. Sheep and cows grazed on pastures in the valley. Tall trees covered the distant hills. It was a sunny day. My friend was in the midst of sharing her story when suddenly I had an experience of oneness with everything I could see. There was no separation, everything was connected. The ground on which I sat, my friend, the valley, the hills, cows and sheep, trees and sky: all were one in my awareness. The experience did not last long, but it was unforgettable.[8]

The man who is free to play and enjoys being playful is drawing from the Lover archetype. Be it golf or tennis, a long walk or a swim, strolling in the woods or fishing in a mountain stream, camping with his family or cruising down the highway in the sports car he always dreamed of having, the Lover enjoys life. Some men are more connected to this energy than others. As Gary shares:

All work and no play makes me a dull boy, a *very* dull boy. I am not focused on one or even two playful activities, but many. I am playful in sexual activity with my wife. I play at imaginary games with my grandchildren. Sometimes I enjoy drawing with crayons. Reading fiction is play time for me. I play in the garden with growing things. I play with my dog. I don't have to build time in to play; I have to build time in to work!

John's play takes him close to the ground. He and his wife have two little boys.

I believe that play is important in my life. Getting the time, though, with two kids is not easy, so their play is very much part of what I do. I spend a lot of time on my knees with them! I think it is important as an adult not to forget that we are all children in some way. A sense of humor is vital too, for example, when our youngest tries to blow out the candles at Sunday Mass when he thinks no one is looking!

I am reminded of Jesus' admonition to his disciples, "I assure you that whoever does not receive the Kingdom of God like a child will never enter it" (Mark 10:15).

Building in quality time for exercise and play can be a challenge. A few years ago I was confronted with this fact when I read the following scripture quote: "Come to me, all of you who are tired of carrying heavy loads, and I will give you rest" (Matthew 11:28). I asked myself, "Where do I find rest?" Then I listed the things I like to do for rest, relaxation, and exercise. Next, I did an honest assessment of what I was *actually* doing. I then was able to make a determination of how to build in more time off.

The Lover is a connoisseur. He loves good food and good wine and takes his time relishing it. I was captivated by Lover energy the day I went to the local Ferrari dealer just to contemplate the elegant Testarossa on display. My friend, Bob, has a Triumph in his garage that he has had for thirty years. Since he only drives it once in a great while, his wife, Patti, has urged him to sell it, but he can't. He's in the grip of the Lover archetype.

Here is Gary again:

> My awareness of God is strongly tied to pleasure. The aroma and flavor of a good cup of coffee immediately makes me God-conscious. A walk on a mountain path, fresh air, and glorious sights are pleasurable and, therefore experiences of God.

Celebrating Eros

Love and sexuality are linked in human experience, though sex is not always born of love and love is not always sexual. With the dignity of each person in mind and the temptations we have to misuse the body, use it irresponsibly, or repress its natural inclinations, let us pause and reflect on the importance of eros.

James Nelson points out rightly, I think, that eros has traditionally received bad press in male-dominated Christian ethics. He writes:

> It has been labeled as egocentric and selfish, something to be suppressed, while agape, self-giving love, has been celebrated as the only genuinely Christian form of love. This, however, is not only questionable theologically and biblically, it is also seriously questionable in regard to psychological health. Men need to affirm and celebrate the eros within. We need to affirm desire as well as self-giving.[9]

To affirm desire is also to affirm the God-given goodness of pleasure. This is not to say we do not need boundaries. It is responsible sexuality, neither unbridled nor repressed, that is implicit here. The Lover needs the other archetypes for true integration and wholeness. So write Moore and Gillette:

> The Lover without boundaries, in his chaos of feeling and sensuality, needs the King to define limits for him, to give him structure, to order his chaos so that it can be channeled creatively. Without limits, the Lover energy turns negative and destructive. The Lover needs the Warrior in order to be able to act decisively, in order to detach, with the clean cut of the sword, from the web of immobilizing sensuality. . . . And the Lover needs the Magician to help him back off from the ensnaring effect of his emotions, in order to reflect, to get a more objective perspective on things, to disconnect—enough at least to see the big picture and to experience the reality beneath the seeming.[10]

In other words, the Magician discerns the Lover's boundaries, the King sets them, and the Warrior defends them.

It is one of life's mysteries that a religion like Christianity, which so profoundly affirms human nature in the Incarnation—Word made *flesh*—has been so negative about the human body and its natural urgings. Perhaps the source of this negativity is fear, the fear of losing control. Perhaps it is the outcome of a dualistic view of the human person, a distinction between one's body and soul rather than the truth of the psychosomatic unity of each person. As Paul Ricoeur explains:

> Suddenly man forgets he is "flesh," indivisibly Word, Desire, and Image; he "knows" himself as a separate Soul, lost and a prisoner in a body; at the

same time he "knows" his body as Other, an evil Enemy.[11]

Contrast this view from what we read in chapter one of Genesis.

God created human beings, making them to be like himself. He created them male and female, blessed them, and said, "Have many children, so that your descendants will live all over the earth. . . ." God looked at everything he had made, and he was very pleased (1:27–28, 31)

In the second chapter of Genesis, the assertion is made that it is not good for man to live alone (2:18). What God is telling us in these biblical quotes is:

◆ Humans are sexual beings by design.

◆ Sexuality (and its genital expression) is good.

◆ One's sexual identity is a reflection of God. We are all made in God's image.

◆ It is in our inter-relationship as sexual beings (but not necessarily in genital activity) that we as men and women fully experience our own wholeness.[12]

Ongoing conversion and an evolution toward sexual maturity, hopefully, is the story of every man. Consider the following two expressions. The first was written by an eighteen-year-old boy and it captures well the desires of a teenager; the second comes from the experience of a man in his late forties who is both a husband and a father:

I want to feel the power of life
to ride it's ferocious pulse
I want to love a beautiful dark-haired woman,
I want to feel her passion
and her desire for me
in both articulate phrases

and in the silent language
of her hands, arms, and lips.
I want to see how much she wants me
every time I look in her eyes.
Even when we are together
she will breathlessly wait for my touch
as I wait for hers.[13]

I feel very comfortable with my sexuality. While, as a teenager and young adult, I based my feelings of physical attraction primarily on a woman's physical appearance, I have come to appreciate that there are many more wonderful dimensions as well. I find myself being attracted to women now whom I would not have even bothered to notice when I was younger. I can see the inner beauty of women and relate to the whole person, not just to surface traits. I have learned how to discriminate between sex and intimacy. I love both men and women and have intimate friendships with some of each. I feel sexually attracted primarily to women, but acknowledge I have felt some sexual attraction to a man on occasion. I restrict sexual interaction, however, to my wife. I have no difficulty with full-body, cheek-to-cheek hugs with both men and women, although I like hugging women more.[14]

I shared earlier the role repression has played in my life. Perhaps it has been a part of your own history too, or maybe you have found yourself acting sexually irresponsibly at times. As a retreat director and confessor, I hear a lot of stories from married people as well as from those living together outside marriage. I hear of happy people who value their affective time together. I listen to men and women who find the amount or quality of their sexual activity a disappointment, even a frustration. Some of these latter tell of being sexually abused as children, others of a puritanical background that has stifled their capacity for sexual pleasure, making them feel shameful of their bodies. The effects of being sexually abused as a child are enormous and devastating, as is well demonstrated in the following statement by the Canadian bishops:

> (This) personal violation causes victims of child sexual abuse to experience many losses . . . including loss of childhood memories, loss of healthy social contact, loss of the opportunity to learn, loss of bodily integrity, loss of identity and self-esteem, loss of trust, loss of sexual maturity and loss of self-determination. All of these personal violations mean that victims of child sexual abuse lose the child's right to a normal childhood. In adulthood it may also mean a loss of the capacity to appreciate sexual intimacy as nurturing, gentle, holy and loving. . . . Many victims experience difficulties related to their sexuality: an inability to enjoy sex or a compulsive desire for sex that may ✓ reflect a confusion about their sexual orientation.[15]

If feeling ashamed of your body is hampering your self-image, you might try the following contemplative prayer exercise.

> Stand naked in front of a full length mirror.
> Consider each part of your body.
> Thank God for those members of your body you value and appreciate.
> Ask God to heal you of any parts of your body that you feel uncomfortable about or ashamed of.
> Repeat this prayer exercise as often as needed until you feel good about being you.

An important experience in my re-awakening to the sacredness of the human body happened during a retreat I was making about ten years ago. It was a healing prayer episode that brought a great deal of inner peace. In it, images came to me of a woman's body. As each image came to my consciousness, I found myself saying, "the beauty of the human body." Then images of my own body appeared. Again I said the words, "the beauty of the human body," as I reflected on each part of my own body. I felt deeply the truth of the beauty of the human body, both male and female. There was no sign of the old fears, no feelings of guilt or self-doubt, just a deep-down peace, and joy for this gift of healing that had been given to me.[16]

When we want to touch and be touched, we are under the influence of the Lover archetype. The most insightful writing I have seen on the value of touch comes from Bernadette Kimmerling, an Irish married woman. In the first of three excellent articles on sexual love and the love of God, she shows how the loving acceptance by another of the truth of the adult body, no matter what this truth may be, or the age of the persons involved, is what allows healing to take place within the self, bringing about self-acceptance. This frees and redeems the other. Her primary focus in the article is on married couples. She writes:

> So the first challenge is to know and accept the adult body, and the most usual method of meeting this challenge is through the physical exchange which occurs in sexual intercourse. Intercourse which takes place within a loving relationship is one powerful way of accepting the physical reality of another. It can be an affirming experience in which each partner, by delighting in the other, reveals to him/her the wholesomeness and beauty of his/her body. Seen through the eyes of the partner, the God-giveness of the human body is revealed. A part of the self which had little meaning in isolation, has its meaning revealed through relationship with another. . . . A part of the self which up until this point may have been marginalized, disowned, fled from, denied or merely tolerated, is now claimed, owned and even

rejoiced in. . . . At the point where the body has been integrated into the personality it can be said to be redeemed.[17]

As a celibate, I have had to come to the redemption of my body by a different route. Yet, arrival at self-acceptance has been accomplished in me as in many other celibate people. An important way this has happened for me has been through hugs. I do not mean the quick, "hello" or "good-bye" kind. I mean when someone holds you. A woman friend of mine, who is happily married, surprised me one day when she told me she found my hugs to be healing for her. I asked her what she meant by this and she replied, "it's because you have no other agenda; it's a free hug." This reminds me of a complaint I sometimes hear from married women: "I wish my husband would just hold me now and then; sometimes I just need to be held."

Obviously, there are many ways to love one's spouse besides having intercourse. In light of this I came across a very interesting pamphlet put together by some high school students in Iowa. It's titled, *101 Ways to Make Love Without Doin' It*.[18] The students were asked to respond in writing to the following question: "If you and your girlfriend or boyfriend had decided to postpone sexual intercourse, how would you let the other person know you loved her or him?" On a weekend retreat for men, most of whom are married, I gave the pamphlet to them and asked each one to circle those activities they did when they first were married and to put a square around those they do now. I asked them to then consider if they wanted to make any changes in their behavior. Here are some of the ways the students suggested.

Tell the other person that you love them ◆ Give or get a hug ◆ Kiss ◆ Hold hands ◆ Walk arm and arm in the woods ◆ Talk openly about your feelings ◆ Exercise together ◆ Sit together in the park ◆ Snuggle up together ◆ Give compliments ◆ Give candy or flowers ◆ Cook a meal together ◆ Gaze at each other ◆ Watch the sunrise together ◆ Flirt with each other ◆ Listen to hurts ◆ Listen to joys ◆ Hide a love note where the other will find it ◆ Talk on the telephone ◆ Make a gift for the other ◆ Make a list of the things you like about each other

James Nelson writes, "A richer, more fulfilling, and more peaceful masculine spirituality will depend in no small measure upon new ways of learning to be sexual."[19] This does not mean a loss in what it means to be male, but a fuller living out of our humanness.

Can we learn the value of relationship from women? The value of mutuality is in satisfying each other's needs for intimacy and for sexual pleasure. "Further," Nelson suggests, "men need more capacity for sexual diffusion—the ability to feel the desire for union throughout the entire body-self, and not simply in the genitals."[20] This comes, in large part, from an appreciation of myself for *who I am* not because of *what I can do* (that is, how well, or not, I perform sexually). "To be a man," notes Nelson, "does not mean to be always in control, always dominant, competitive, and emotionally invulnerable. It means to be a male human being—with distinctive male sexual experience and energy, but also with unique capacities for the whole range of human traits."[21] I may need to learn to love the "body-self" that I am. This is part of the redemptive process of owning in myself, through God's grace, the truth of the Incarnation, that my body-self has been raised to a new level of dignity by the Second Person of the Trinity becoming human.

The heart is like a garden. It needs to be cultivated. The weeds of selfishness, repression, and fear have to be removed if the flowers of freedom are to grow. It requires fertilization, frequent doses of love received and given. The gardener must learn to be patient, for it takes time for the seed to open, to sprout, to become a new creation. Sometimes it is quiet in the garden; one can almost hear the stalks breaking ground. At other times the chirping of birds and the sound of bees at work let the gardener know that his creation is alive and thriving. The heart can be a lively place.

In the movie, *Dances With Wolves,* we witness the slow but steady growth of John Dunbar as his heart first opens to the Native people. We watch him as he gradually falls in love with Stands-With-a-Fist and ultimately marries her. We marvel at the transition in the heart of the brave, Wind-in-His-Hair, who starts out suspicious of Dunbar and eventually becomes his friend. My heart is stirred whenever I watch this movie, for toward the end, as Dunbar and his wife and their child leave the tribe, a shout rises from the mountain. It is the Brave yelling out to John Dunbar, "Can you see that you will always be my friend!" This movie captures the three kinds of love—*eros, agape,* and *amor*—brilliantly.

The False Lover

We have seen in this chapter examples of the good lover and of the false lover. The false lover is exhibited in sensually addictive behavior, without boundaries, without respect for oneself or for others, He is caught up in a whirlwind of unending pleasure, lost in sensuality. He is possessed by the very energy that could free him. He is off-center. The false lover is never satisfied, always longing for another sensual delight. He is a glutton, a bottomless pit. He overeats, overdrinks, overdoes anything pleasurable. Moderation is not in his vocabulary. He must learn the values of discipline, of a healthy asceticism, of the necessity of setting boundaries or he will drown in a sea of sensuality.

The false lover also manifests himself in impotence. He does not feel. He is lacking in enthusiasm, living a passionless life. Here is the affective "couch potato," distanced from reality, from family and friends. He may be chronically depressed. He is unable to have an intimate relationship because he is not in touch with his feelings. The man in the grip of this version of the false lover does not have a satisfactory sex life if one at all. He needs to recapture the fire he has lost.

Jesus said, "I have come to light a fire on the earth. How I wish the blaze were ignited!" (Luke 12:49 NAB). A traditional prayer to the Holy Spirit has us ask to be inflamed with love, "Come Holy Spirit, fill the hearts of your faithful with the *fire* of your love (emphasis mine)."

Two of Jesus' disciples, on their way home after his crucifixion, disappointed and depressed at what had happened in Jerusalem, found their hearts rekindled by a conversation with a stranger. They said to one another, "Wasn't it like a fire burning in us when he talked to us on the road and explained the scriptures to us?" (Luke 24:32) Without hesitating, they *turned around* (a symbol of conversion) and headed back to Jerusalem now full of joy and enthusiasm. They experienced the power of the resurrection, a love-energy available to us too. All we have to do is ask God for it. This has been my experience many times.

If your spiritual life needs a shot in the arm, if your fire of passion and compassion has nearly been extinguished, if your zest for life is waning, go to the Lord, go to the Spirit, and ask for a resurgence of lover energy. Do so in your own words or beseech God as this African Christian has:

O God:
Enlarge my heart
that it may be big enough to receive the
greatness of your love.
Stretch my heart
that it may take into it all those who
with me around the world
believe in Jesus Christ.
Stretch it
that it may take into it all those who
do not know him,
but who are my responsibility because

I know him.
And stretch it
that it may take in all those who are not
lovely in my eyes,
and whose hands I do not want to touch;
through Jesus Christ, my savior, Amen.[22]

Questions for Reflection

As we seek to access the fullness of the Lover's energy, the following questions are offered as an aid in this process.

1. Were your parents affectionate with one another? Did their behavior affect your affectivity: towards your wife, your children, and good friends?

2. How do you feel about your body? Do you appreciate it, take care of it? Are there any members of your body you dislike or feel ashamed of?

   Are you in touch with your feelings? With your senses?

3. Is it easy or difficult for you to be weak or vulnerable with those you love?

4. If you are married, in what ways do you see Christ in your wife? Do you like as well as love her? How do you show your love to her?

5. Would you say you have a general passion for life? How does this manifest itself, for example, by savoring a delicious meal, delighting in play, being alive to music, art, or poetry, being an inventive lover, or in other ways.

   Are you able to feel with others in their pain?

6. Are there any habits of the false lover in you? Are you, for example, lacking in affective boundaries, caught in a whirlwind of unending pleasure, lost in sensuality, gluttonous with food, drink, sex, gambling, whatever. . . ? Or are you

impotent in regard to life: not in touch with your feelings or your senses, repressed in your sexuality, lacking compassion for the wounded of the world, both the people and the planet living a passionless life?

SEVEN

Dealing with Father Wounds

Among a man's jobs is to reclaim his own grief. When a man has reclaimed his grief and investigated his wound, he may find that they resemble the grief and the wound his father had, and the reclaiming puts him in touch with his father's soul.

—Robert Bly

My father died one month short of his eightieth birthday, in the summer of 1990. Preaching at his funeral Mass was one of the most difficult tasks I have ever faced. In fact, I rewrote the homily three times.

My father had a split personality, or so it seemed to me as a child. On the one hand, he could be charming, witty, fun to be with, and affectionate. Yet without warning, he could be sarcastic, angry, and put me down in front of my friends. It was a cause of confusion and, it took its toll on his children. I came out of the situation with a low self-image, an inferiority complex, and an inability to express anger.

When I was a young Jesuit, I remember seeing the movie *David and Lisa*, about two troubled teenagers who meet in a mental institution. It was a powerful movie for me in many ways, but the scene and the message that had the most impact upon me was during one of the counseling sessions David had with his psychiatrist. David was railing against something his parents had done to him as a child. The psychiatrist said to him, "David, your parents have a right to be fallible." That sentence jumped right into my head. Like David, I had been operating on the false assumption that my parents could do no wrong. My eyes began to open to a reality I had never considered before that day.

Let us return to the funeral for my father. On the evening before the Rosary, my sisters and brother and I gathered in the family living room to share how we felt about Dad and about his death. We live far apart from one another and there is the added distance of age: my brother and I are seventeen years apart, the three girls in between. I am the eldest. Our mother died at an early age; I was twenty years old when she passed away. Each of us children has had different experiences with Dad, some positive, some negative. Some of these incidents had become common knowledge, others were shared for the first time that evening. Lots of emotions were expressed: sadness, a sense of loss of an important figure in our lives, anger over past hurts, dismay over his seemingly split-personality and its effects on us, and joy that Dad had finally found his place of peace. We also explored the *why* of the negative side to his personality. He was very successful in business, what one of my siblings termed, "a self-made man." But because of our experience of him, we came to the conclusion that Dad never really loved himself, that his put-downs were his way of building up his own self-image. This, we believe, he did, in a mostly unconscious way.

Without benefit of psychological counseling, he continued this behavior without seeming to realize the harm he was doing, the emotional wounds he was inflicting. (It is important to point out that the wounds a man may experience as a child can also come from his mother and that these need to be dealt with as well in order to achieve emotional maturity.) In my homily at Dad's funeral Mass, I recognized this personality defect of Dad when I said:

> Each of us, his children, remember Dad in our own way. We remember the love he gave us as well as the hurts. We recall the good times we had with him as well as the difficult moments. We know he loved us the best way he knew how.

I made an important discovery at the age of twenty-eight: to become an adult in my family, one had to face my father in a confrontational way. Finally I was able to do this, but only after undergoing a year's worth of counseling. During that time I learned, among other things, to feel anger and to express it appropriately. My father would not allow me to express my anger as a child, so I repressed it. I did manage to confront him once when I was in high school, but I got thrown out of the house as a result. So it wasn't until five years after I joined the Jesuits that I finally had the tools necessary to stand up to him. I was nervous on that day of our reckoning, but confront him I did. The feeling was exhilarating and freeing. What happened afterwards was unexpected; we became friends. This friendship grew and lasted the rest of his life. We still had our occasional disagreements and, both being of Italian descent, our angry airing of different points of view, but we learned how to listen to one another and how to apologize to each other. I gradually came to understand him better and to love him in spite of his faults. Thus, I was able to say in my homily at the funeral Mass:

> St. Paul reminds us that nothing can separate us from the love of God (Romans 8:35-39). Neither our sins nor our faults, no matter how great, can separate us from God's love. Neither did Dad's fears and insecurities separate him from God's unconditional love, nor from our love either. We love Dad the best way we know how.

With this understanding of how my father and I became friends, the reader will likely be as surprised as I was at what happened to me after he died.

One year later, during the summer, I saw a video called, *A Gathering of Men*.[1] It was an interview by Bill Moyers with Robert Bly, the poet and author of the book *Iron John*. He is the founding father of what is known as the men's movement. I was very touched by some of Bly's insights. Unexpectedly, they connected me to some unfinished business between me and Dad. I thought I had worked through all the bad stuff in relation to him. But evidently, there were some hurts buried deep in my subconscious that had not yet been healed. These emotional wounds needed a stimulus to unlock them. As it turned out, the video opened a door.

Bly discussed how men have a sense of loss, confusion, and grief over the absence of their fathers. This absence began with the Industrial Revolution when the father went out of the house to work.

> When your father is away during the day and during the year, when he only comes home at five o'clock (or later), you only get his temperament. What you used to get was his teaching and his temperament.[2]

He's tired from work, gets irritable easily, is more susceptible to being impatient or even getting angry. His dark side emerges: "Do your homework!" "Don't bother me; I'm reading the newspaper!" "Obey your mother!" and on it goes. When he has a good day at work, we breathe a sigh of relief.

The second consequence of this absence, which also stems from the Industrial Revolution, is the loss of the father's teaching. Because the father is away all day, the son does not receive any knowledge of what the complete male mode of feeling is. Before, the son received something from his father by standing close to him in his shop, at his craft. Here is Bly:

When we stand physically close to our father, some-thing—something moves over that can't be described in material terms, that gives the son a cer-tain confidence, an awareness, a knowledge of what it is to be male, what a man is. And in the ancient times you were always with your father; he taught you how to do things, he taught you how to farm, he taught you whatever it is that he did. You learned from him.[3]

when I was a child I like to go to the store when Dad worked and slice the high school... watch him work

I have friends in Ireland who own a farm. I admire the relationship between the father and his son, the transfer not only of knowledge but also of a sense of the land, of the sea-sons, and what it takes to make one's living from the earth. My father actually did hand on to me a feel for the food business as I worked for him occasionally and he affirmed my part-time job as a box boy and then as a clerk at the local supermarket.

Bly maintains that an important door to male feeling is grief. This is so, because in our culture, boys are taught not to cry. It is part of our social conditioning that boys are dis-couraged from crying while girls who cry are considered sensitive and caring. The problem is when we do not let go of control (hard for men to do) and directly, or indirectly, feel our loss, our hurt, our pain, these feelings are being repressed. Dr. Alan Wolfelt, Director of the Center for Loss and Life Transition, explains:

As the boy moves toward becoming a man he is taught to behave in certain acceptable "masculine" ways. Acknowledging feelings of loss in this context results in feelings of vulnerability and uncomfort-ableness. . . . This social conditioning process of glo-rified masculinity creates a major impediment to a male's expression of grief.[4]

However, as we shall see, in order to be healed of hurts, whether from a father or mother, a man must descend into his grief. It is grief for what he did not get from his father, legitimate needs which were not met: affection, affirmation, encouragement, his presence, whatever it may be. Another way of describing this is "the wound a son receives from his father."[5] It is very important to have someone to talk to during the healing process: a psychologist, grief counselor, or good friend with some training in counseling.

Of all that I heard on the video, this insight on loss and grief had the biggest impact on me because I was beginning to realize that I had not yet fully been healed of all the hurts from my past. This gave me a direction in which to go for that healing. D. H. Lawrence expressed it well:

> I am not a mechanism, an assembly of various sections.
> And it is not because the mechanism is working wrongly, that I am ill.
> I am ill because of wounds to the soul, to the deep emotional self—
> and the wounds to the soul take a long, long time, only time can help
> and patience, and a certain difficult repentance
> long difficult repentance, realization of life's mistake, and the freeing oneself
> from the endless repetition of the mistake. . . . [6]

It had been a long, long time since I had received the wounds to my soul. I was fifty-two years old the summer I saw the interview of Robert Bly. I had faced my low self-image years ago and, with God's help, had slowly worked out of that hole. Perhaps this is the "repentance" that D. H. Lawrence writes of. Someone in the family has to break the chain or the sins of the father will not only be visited on the son, but also, through him, to his own children. The mistake will be endlessly repeated until someone says, "Stop! I want to be healed and I am willing to do what is necessary for the healing to happen."

All the writers in the men's movement that I have read insist that young men need a mentor to initiate them from boyhood into manhood. For some, this wisdom figure comes in the guise of one's father-in-law, for others a friend of the family or one's boss at work. For the young priest, it may be his pastor, or bishop. Thank God one of the greatest gifts I received as a young Jesuit was mentors, older Jesuits who helped me to believe in myself and to discover academic and personality attributes that were buried in me. They helped me to believe in myself. They helped me to break the chain of low self-esteem that I had inherited from my father.

The seriousness of debilitating father wounds took on new meaning for me a couple of years ago while I was leading a men's weekend. One of the men shared that he was unable to learn how to read and write until he was an adult. This was because his father, an alcoholic, and a violent one at that, would frequently stop at the local bar on his way home from work. He would arrive home at the same time that his children were attempting to do their homework. When they heard him coming toward the house, they became so frightened they could not study.

During the summer following my father's death, as I reflected on the insights I gained from the interview of Robert Bly, I came to the realization that if I was to get past blaming Dad for childhood hurts, I had to grieve whatever losses still remained in my memory. I knew, too, that if I was to have a more compassionate understanding of my father, the kind that could eventually forgive him for the ways he had wounded me, I had to do the necessary inner work to bring this about. It was at this juncture that the catalyst for this healing arrived on the scene.

Enter a man older than myself who was in a position of authority. Every time I was in his presence, I felt uncomfortable. At first I did not know why. I shared my feelings with a close friend. He had met my father and knew some of our history. My friend exclaimed: "This is about you and your Dad! This isn't about you and Jim! Jim's behavior is reminding you of some of the ways your father acted. Don't waste your time reacting to Jim. Let his negative actions help you to bring up memories from your childhood that still need healing. When Jim acts badly towards you, focus your attention on the like ways you were treated by your father and grieve." I realized, as my friend was speaking, that I was being given a golden opportunity for deeper healing and wholeness. I said yes to whatever this process would involve.

First, I made a commitment to spend as much time as I could with Jim. I did this even though I knew I was asking for the cross. I would take appropriate breaks so as not to overload my psyche. Second, I determined not to react to his negative behavior; I would keep my focus on my Dad. Third, I kept in touch with my friend who listened to me as I related the latest incident with Jim and what memory it brought up from my past. My friend was especially helpful in encouraging me to keep my focus on my father and not react to Jim's behavior.

I thanked God for so providentially placing Jim in my life at this time. I prayed for courage to face the wounds of the past. Psalm 27 spoke directly to what I was going through:

The Lord is my light and my salvation;
I will fear no one [I added, "and no thing"].
The Lord protects me from all danger;
I will never be afraid (Ps 27:1)

I asked God for patience in the process of healing my father wounds. Again, I drew strength from Psalm 27,

Wait for the Lord with courage;
be stouthearted and wait for the Lord (Ps 27:14 NAB).

Often, the daily Mass readings spoke to my heart: of God's presence in my trial, of the necessity of carrying the cross involved in dredging up old memories, to depend on God for the strength to continue, and so forth.

I am one of those men who was taught as a boy not to cry; I do so rarely. Occasionally, however, during this time of grieving—a process which took over four months—I actually was able to shed tears. Sometimes I awakened in the middle of the night and recalled a dream in which I was crying over something. Once I recall sobbing in a dream. While I was letting painful memories surface on the conscious level, the unconscious was evidently doing its work too.

I kept a journal, noting especially those times when a breakthrough occurred—an encounter with Jim, a memory that surfaced, how I was able to grieve. Words from Robert Bly and other authors on masculine psychology continued to inspire and help me.[7]

One particular passage from Bly's book, *Iron John*, motivated me. It is the same quote I used to begin this chapter, but it bears repeating here.

> Among a man's jobs is to reclaim his own grief. When a man has reclaimed his grief and investigated his wound, he may find that they resemble the grief and the wound his father had, and the reclaiming puts him in touch with his father's soul.

Bly adds, "Once his senses are sharpened, he will be able to smell the father's wound."[8] I now know what caused my father to have his low self-image. The *why* of it is not the same as the cause of mine, but the effect was the same. By getting in touch with these last memories of my wound and by being able to grieve, I eventually came to the outcome I had hoped for from the beginning: I forgave my father. This is such a good feeling, an experience of freedom, one of joy and peace, a deep inner peace.

Although the healing of the memories lasted four months, it took another seven months before I knew I had changed. During the whole eleven months, I was engaged in my retreat ministry; this took up a lot of my energy. It was during my annual eight-day retreat when I had time to pause from my busy schedule and reflect back on the previous year, that I realized I was a different person. On that retreat, the graces of healing came together into a sense of wholeness.

Besides the inner sense of peace I received from finally being able to forgive my father for his mistakes, the healing had other effects. First of all, I noticed I was relating with men more easily. Older men, in particular, started asking me for advice. Secondly, one of the insights I had received during my encounters with Jim was that I was still hampered by a fear of male anger. This, even though I had confronted my father many times as an adult. Like my father, Jim had a temper and I never knew when or what would set him off. I had faced Jim's anger and had learned how not to be intimidated by it. In male-archetype language, I had accessed my Warrior energy more fully. I experienced a new assertiveness within myself that has affected all my relationships and even my ministry. A new source of strength was set free within me.

There comes a time in a man's life when he must face the demons of his past in order to achieve maturity. Whether his wound comes from his father or his mother or from some significant other person in his childhood, he will not be fully free until this process of healing happens. I hope that, by sharing from my story, the reader will find the way, if he hasn't already, to his own greater wholeness.

EIGHT

Conclusion

The unexamined life is not worth living.

—Socrates

What we call the beginning is often the end
And to make an end is to make a beginning.
The end is where we start from.

—T.S. Eliot

In the course of this book we have considered a variety of ways to reflect on our life experiences. One such way, mentioned earlier, is called the Consciousness Examen. Sometimes known as the Awareness Examen, the Consciousness Examen is composed of five steps:

1. Thanksgiving
2. Petition
3. Reflection on the Day
4. Contrition
5. Looking to the Future

The Examen is more than an examination of conscience, a practice Catholics learn as a prelude to receiving the sacrament of reconciliation, or confession. The Examen helps us to find God more clearly in our daily lives. It is a means to help us learn what God wants of us. And it is an effective way to get to know ourselves better, including both our strengths and weaknesses.

The main concern in the Consciousness Examen is to learn how God is affecting and moving us deep in our affective consciousness.[1] This is a challenging concept for many men because it means being in touch with one's feelings. However, if we are to truly live out the values of our faith—honesty, integrity, generosity, compassion, tolerance, patience, and responsibility—with family and friends, at work, in all our activities, then we need to be aware of the emotions which help and hinder these endeavors.

The Examen is a form of prayer. One can do it on a daily basis or at the end of the week. It is best to practice the Examen in a quiet place and at the time of day or night when one is most alert.

The first step is Thanksgiving. I begin the exercise by giving thanks to God for loving me unconditionally and everlastingly. I reflect on the ways I have experienced love: from my spouse, my children, a good friend, etc. I thank God for my good health and for the care I receive when I am sick. I express gratitude for having a job, a roof over my head, enough money to meet the basic needs of life. I may even wish to thank God for the crosses in my life, for it is often through them that I become a better person. The Examen helps me, in St. Ignatius of Loyola's words, to "find God in all things," that is, in the particular circumstances of my life. It is an exercise of my faith, for it looks at daily events in the light of faith.

The second step of the Examen involves asking God for help. For example, I may ask to have eyes to see all the ways the Spirit is present in my life, or I may ask help to live more fully my true self. Recall Joseph Campbell's definition of the Hero: "the man who has battled past his own limitations to become fully human." I ask God to help me see how his supportive grace has helped me to transcend my weaknesses and fears in the living out of my faith. I ask to know if I have been blind to God's presence in any way.

Step three is a reflection on the day (or week). Since the Examen is a form of prayer, it is not simply a matter of my natural powers of memory and analysis as I review the day. As George Aschenbrenner explains, "It is a matter of Spirit-guided insight into my life and courageously responsive sensitivity to God's call in my heart."[2]

God and I are on this journey together. Thus, I review the day, moment by moment, circumstance by circumstance, reflecting on the persons I was in contact with. Was God saying anything to me? How did I respond? How well did I succeed in living out my values? Then I give thanks for the times when I was true to my beliefs. And I consider any times that I failed to love or was unable to appreciate another's love for me. While doing this step, I may discover an aspect of my false self that needs special attention. Perhaps I may need to be more sensitive to the needs of my wife or more attentive to the problems my children are encountering, or possibly I realize I need to grow more in living out the courage of my convictions at work. Awareness of my need for conversion, for a change in attitude and behavior, is not done in order to feel guilty, but as necessary groundwork for transformation. It is good to remember that I do this self-evaluation in the presence of God's all-encompassing love, this God, who in the words of the Psalmist, "understands my thoughts from afar" (Psalm 139:2 NAB) and in whose eyes I am "precious and glorious" (Isaiah 43:4 NAB). My desire is to be a more loving person, of God, of myself, of others.

Contrition, or sorrow for the ways I did not act out of love today, is the fourth step in the Examen. This step is a prayer for forgiveness and healing. The four male archetypes offer a good model for reflection here. I examine how I am living out the false King, Warrior, Magician, or Lover. I ask God to heal me of the root causes of these failings and to give me the strength to live, instead, the fullness of each archetype: to be a good King, an honest Warrior, a compassionate Magician, and a responsible Lover. The sorrow expressed here is not from shame, nor a cause for depression. It is a faith experience, steeped in trust in God's mercy. It is an invitation to live more deeply the love that God has placed in my heart.

The final step in the Consciousness Examen points me in the direction of the future, and leads me to look forward with hope. It is important to integrate what lies ahead into my life. I do this by placing any anxieties or worries about the future in God's hands.

I ask God to help me face the future without fear or self-doubt. I ask God to help me be more sensitive to the subtle ways in which the divine presence is in my daily life and to have the courage to respond to the divine invitations to love with greater magnanimity and consistency. With St. Paul, I am in pursuit of a holy goal:

> I keep striving to win the prize for which Christ Jesus has already won me to himself. Of course, my brothers (and sisters), I really do not think that I have already won it; the one thing I do, however, is to forget what is behind me and do my best to reach what is ahead. So I run straight ahead toward the goal in order to win the prize, which is God's call through Christ Jesus to the life above (Philippians 3:12-14).

And so I surrender any fears of the future to God's providential love and simply offer the coming day, or week, to God. I offer the difficult moments as well as the coming joys and ask that God be in each and that I may recognize his presence in each. I may also wish to ask God's grace for that particular area of my life that is in need of conversion.

There is no specific time frame in which to make each of the five steps of the Consciousness Examen. As George Aschenbrenner explains, "At one time we are drawn to one element longer than the others and at another time to another element over the others."[3] The important thing is get in touch with the "mood of my heart."

When first practicing this form of reflection on our faith life, it may seem formal and mechanical, but as we learn to integrate what we are feeling and experiencing it flows more easily. The primary purpose of the Examen is ultimately to develop both a listening heart and a discerning vision. These are to be active not just during the fifteen or so minutes of the exercise, but continually.[4]

Peace is a basic desire of the human heart. The Consciousness Examen is one way to attain this state as we learn how to find God in the ordinary events of our life. The Examen enables us to become attuned to our interior feelings, moods, and inner urgings. It implies that we are not frightened by them, nor do we consider this to be just "women's work." Rather, we have learned to take what is going on within us seriously. What follows is an example of how to do the five steps:

Thanksgiving

Good and gracious God, I rejoice in your love for me. You thought of me and so loved the idea of me that you caused me to be. Each moment you are at work loving me into existence. Thank you for loving me and accepting me as I am. Thank you for all the ways you have blessed me; for my family and friends who have supported and loved me. Thank you for my life this day, for my body, for the ability to see, to hear, to walk and speak. Thank you for all my talents, especially for my ability to learn, to make choices, and to love. Most of all I thank you for your Son, Jesus, who died that I might have life. Thank you for the gift of your Spirit who guides me in my journey to closer union with you. Thank you for the ways I am coming to know myself better and for the ways I am coming to know and love you more.

Petition for Light

God of love and mercy, you know me better than I know myself. Please help me to become more aware of how you have been working in my presence during the past hours (days). I wish to respond more fully to your invitations to live a good, moral life, and with greater faithfulness. I can do this only to the degree I recognize your guidance. Help me then to become more sensitive to your Spirit's direction and more conscious of the ways I fail to respond. I place this time of prayerful reflection in your hands.

Reflection of the Day

What has been happening to me? How has God been working in me? What has God been asking of me? I let my mind go quietly over the different phases of my day. What feelings did I experience? What thoughts or reflections moved me, positively or negatively? Do these movements tell me anything about how God is working in my life and what God is asking of me? How have I responded? Is there any specific aspect of my false self that needs attention? I reflect on the day with these or other questions and discuss them with God.

Sorrow for My Faults

Merciful and compassionate God, thank you for your care and guidance during these past hours (days). Thank you for all the ways I was aware of, and responded to, the promptings of the Holy Spirit. I am truly sorry for the times I was not sensitive to your invitations and for the ways I failed to respond faithfully. You have been so good to me; I want to respond with acts of love. You know me. You know the areas in my life that are in need of healing and forgiveness. I place myself before you and ask you to strengthen me through Jesus Christ, your Son. Thank you. I trust in your power and your love.

Looking to the Future

Provident God, I look to the future with hope. You accept me the way I am and invite me to grow. You give me time and opportunity and grace. I place the time between now and my next Examen in your hands. I ask you to help me be more sensitive and responsive to the Spirit's presence and guidance. (Here you might reflect a bit on the coming events and talk with God about your feelings.) I ask your special help in those areas of my personality most in need of conversion. Loving God, with the Spirit in my heart, I go forward with joy and trust. Amen.

Eleanor Roosevelt was quoted as saying, "You must do the thing you think you cannot do." As you consider the theme of this book, the art of reflective living, what is it you think you cannot do? Which of Nicholas Harnan's four suggestions for living reflectively is especially difficult for you: slowing down in order to have time to reflect; getting beyond the surface level of your life to a deeper order in reality; staying with an experience, even a painful one, in order to plumb its deeper meaning; or sharing your intimate thoughts and feelings with a trusted friend? Is the exercise of reflecting on your life a new experience for you? If so, a good way to begin is by keeping a journal.

KEEPING A JOURNAL

A major goal in life is to become a well-integrated person, for as the great Saint Irenaeus pointed out, "The glory of God is people fully alive." The practice of maintaining a journal can assist you in your personal adventure towards wholeness. A journal has many uses:

◆ Helps identify direction and potentiality.

◆ Crystallizes decisions that need to be made.

◆ Enables us to know ourselves better.

◆ Identifies new goals to work toward.

◆ Helps test whether we are doing what we planned (like working on a particular aspect of our false self).

◆ Helps us to process events and see patterns in our lives.

This method of reflecting on one's life may not appeal to everyone. As an extrovert, I find keeping a journal an excellent means of processing what goes on in the ordinary events of my life, of seeing God's presence in them, and discovering ways to more fully integrate the four basic archetypes. I have been doing this reflective exercise since I was a Jesuit novice. Sometimes I write in my journal on a daily basis, other times at the end of a week or at a significant time in my life. Every six weeks I review what I have written since the last evaluation in order to see how I have grown, both psychologically and spiritually. I am especially interested in noting how I have grown into a fuller living out of my true self, for example, by reaching a new level of compassion, taking the initiative to mend a broken or injured relationship, facing and overcoming a temptation, or achieving a greater sensitivity to God's loving presence in my life.

Journaling helps me to fulfill all four of Harnan's suggestions because I share a summary of what I have written every six weeks with my spiritual director. Like the Consciousness Examen, taking the time to keep a journal helps me keep in touch with my inner journey, both my feelings and my thoughts.

There are different ways to record the events of one's daily life in written form:

An Ordinary Journal: writing down those aspects of my life that have personal significance, though not necessarily in reference to God.

A Diary: a chronological account of my daily activities.

The Intensive Journal: so-called by Ira Progoff who created it. Like a psychological workbook, the concern of the Intensive Journal is the transformation of one's psyche to a more healthy level. It is a means of reaching a direct contact with the creative principle that is at the core of life. By intensely focusing personal depth experience, it is designed to bring about a breakthrough in awareness and a recognition of the inner direction and meaning of the individual's inner life.[5]

A Spiritual Journal: keeping track of what is happening in my faith life. I record my feelings: joy, grief, fear, anger, anxieties, guilt, etc. I also record images, and thoughts in light of my faith and my relationship with God. This is the kind of journal I maintain.

Looking over the last year I notice a variety of topics I wrote about. There are scripture passages that connected directly to something I was undergoing, for example, calling to God for help by using one of the Psalms (Psalms 5, 6, 25, 57, 69, 86, 102, etc.), finding patience in the midst of a struggle from Psalm 27: "Wait for the Lord with courage; be stouthearted, and wait for the Lord" (verse 14, NAB), and putting into words something deep in my heart when I was feeling overwhelmed by the extent of my ministries: "I cannot carry all this people by myself, for they are too heavy for me" (Numbers 11:14, NAB). I found mentioned graces I received from God and an account of how I responded to them. There are prayers of gratitude to God for the blessings in my life. My journal has in it experiences of God in my prayer and ways God freed me from aspects of my false self. Finally, there are recounted various conversion experiences I witnessed in people who attended the retreats I gave, sources of hope for my own journey.

One of the goals of St. Ignatius of Loyola was to "find God in all things." I am intensely interested in the adventure of knowing and experiencing God as much as possible. The spiritual journal has been a great help in this endeavor.

Reflective Themes

The following are some general themes and accompanying questions that one might attend to in keeping a spiritual journal. Perhaps taking one theme at a time, one a week, or one a month, would be a good way to get in the habit of reflecting on one's faith journey.

Self-Knowledge

What am I grateful for: a blessing, good health, family, friends, my faith, anything?

What brings me joy and happiness, pain and sorrow?

In what ways do I need to grow emotionally or spiritually to be more of a loving person—toward myself, my spouse, my children, grandchildren, friends, coworkers, etc.?

What are my anxieties and fears, worries and concerns, desires and hopes?

How well am I coping with life's difficulties? What do I need to respond better?

Are there any ways in which I am a slave to my needs, to my false King, Warrior, Magician, or Lover?

What are the characteristics of my true self—my good qualities, virtues, and so forth?

How have I grown personally and spiritually since I last wrote in my journal?

Experience of Faith in General

What is my image of God: loving, forgiving, judging, condemning?

Has this image changed over the years?

Who is Jesus for me: friend, companion, shepherd, model?

How do I experience the work of the Holy Spirit in my life?

Where in my life do I realize letting go of control, surrender, deep trust in God? Do I need to improve in this?

What are the crosses in my life?

Am I able to see them as a blessing instead of as a curse?

Am I in a spiritual oasis or in a desert, a dark time?

Experience of Communal Faith

How do I experience myself as loved by others?

Do I resist this love in any way?

How do I experience myself as loving others?

How have I have been compassionate to those in need?

Have I discovered any prejudices in my heart, for example, toward those who are homeless, on welfare, unemployed, undocumented, suffering from AIDS, and so forth?

Do I stand up for what is right, honest, and just when the opportunities present themselves? I recount the times I have or haven't.

Are there any relationships in my life that need healing, reconciling?

How can I become a more effective peacemaker?[6]

Experience of Faith in My Work Environment

How do I live out gospel values of honesty, integrity, compassion, and courage where I work?

Do I identify what I am doing with Christ in my work situation, for example, as consoler, healer, challenger, shepherd?

Have I made any professional decisions that were not congruent with what I believe is right?

How do I experience God's presence in my work environment?

Am I using my God-given talents to the best of my ability; what would need to change for this to happen more completely?

CARING FOR YOUR SOUL

Thomas Moore is best known for his thought-provoking book, *Care of the Soul: A Guide for Cultivating Depth and Sacredness in Everyday Life*. Caring for our souls is an effort to see the most ordinary of our activities as full of meaning and nourishment. Moore explains what he means by soul: "Soul is not a thing, but a quality or a dimension of experiencing life and ourselves. It has to do with depth, value, relatedness, heart, and personal substance. I do not use the word here as an object of religious belief or as something to do with immortality."[7] Caren Goldman has nicely put together ten of Moore's suggestions for practicing "care of the soul."

1. *Nourish and educate your imagination.* The mind thinks; the soul imagines. Reading, listening to stories, exposing yourself to all the arts are ways of caring for the soul. The stuff of the world is there to be made into images that become tabernacles of spirituality and containers of mystery.

2. *Respond to what asks to be dealt with.* Take what is most pressing at the moment. You don't have to look around for something else to do. The most pressing thing can be as complicated as a relationship, but it can also be as simple as a door falling off a hinge. Soul is affected by the small details and tiny decisions of everyday life.

3. *Listen to your heart.* We avoid caring for the soul when we have superficial, ready-made explanations for what is going on in our lives. The soul is poetic. There is never one story that will explain everything. Simple explanations of our pain can keep the soul from flourishing, no matter how compelling the story behind them.

4. *Learn to live with complexity.* To care for the soul, we must live with complexity instead of running from it. Ask the question, "How do I distance myself from the problems and challenges in my life?" Is it by not using my talents and gifts? By not being able to live without knowing? By

avoiding paradox and mystery? Care of the soul does not offer the illusion of a problem-free life. The poet John Keats says the point is to "feel" existence.

5. *Live an individual life.* Be willing to go against the grain of the establishment. This might mean becoming more eccentric, or even being irrational. Recognize that care of the soul results in an individual "I" that you may never have planned for.

6. *Choose work that suits the soul, as well as the budget.* Explore the "soul values" of your potential work place. What is its spirit? Will I be treated as a person here? Is there a feeling of community here? Do people love their work? Are there any moral or ethical problems? It is not possible to care for the soul while violating one's own moral sensibilities.

7. *Be of service to others.* Recognize that the soul exists beyond your personal circumstances and conceptions. You are well on the way toward soul when you feel attachment to your family, community, and the world.

8. *Learn that the soul speaks through simple things.* Recognize the soul speaking in your home furnishing, in architecture, in mountains and lakes, in boarded-up houses and crime-ridden streets—in everything around you. In the area of anima mundi (soul of the world), there is no separation between the individual soul and the world's soul.

9. *Know your own mythology. Mythology is not the same as myth.* It is a collection of stories that attempt to portray the myths, the deep patterns, that we live out in our everyday life. Our memories, reflections, and dreams are all rich with imagination and soul. As we reflect on our experiences and learn to express them artfully, we are making life more soulful.

10. *Be exposed to spirituality in a soulful way.* The emphasis here is on images and stories instead of high spiritual achievement. Discover many different spiritual traditions and let them teach you how to make ritual part of your everyday life. Ritual is an action that speaks to the heart and soul but does not necessarily make sense in a literal way. By letting go of more and more of what Jungians call the dominant function—our primary mode of relating with life—we can give more care to the soul every day.[8]

Moore's suggestions are excellent pointers toward a fuller, more reflective life. Recall that reflection enables us to see reality anew. With his emphasis on the value of the imagination, Moore helps us to understand our experiences in a deeper, more profound way.

Final Word

There are many ways to stimulate our powers of reflection. In this book we have considered a variety of methods to facilitate personal integration and wholeness. Whether one follows the guidance of Sam Keen as he explains the Soulful Quest,[1] the Vision Quest of Native Americans, Joseph Campbell's Hero's journey, or Carl Jung's four basic male archetypes, the guiding theme of the book is that, in the words of Socrates, "the unexamined life is not worth living." As human beings we have the ability to use both our rational and intuitive faculties to help us become better persons by coming in touch with the deepest, truest, dimension of ourselves. We have examined many of the ways to do this: reflective questions (such as those proposed in the questionnaire at the beginning of the book), journaling, the Consciousness Examen, reading biblical passages for personal meaning, and reflecting on father/mother wounds. Whatever methods one chooses, the main thing is to stay in touch with the deeper meaning in life.

I close with this marvelous quote from Rabbi Abraham Heschel.

> From without, I may seem to be quite average and ordinary, but from within, through self-reflection, I see myself as unique, precious, unprecedented; I am not to be exchanged for anything else. Beyond the distress and anxiety and busy-ness of life lies this most fundamental aspect of self-reflection: I am of great moment, I am an original, not a copy.[2]

NOTES

INTRODUCTION

1. Here are the seven issues and the questions accompanying each. Each respondent answered in essay form.

Work: Do you find your work satisfying? How much of your identity is in your work? What ethics do you bring to your job?

Play: Is it important in your life? In what ways do you play? Do you build in enough time for play?

Intimacy: Describe. In your relationships, especially with your wife, children, grandchildren, your parents, male and female friends. Intimacy as self-disclosure, do you find it easy or difficult to share your feelings with others?

Prayer: Time you allow for prayer on a daily, weekly, basis. What ways do you like to pray? Do you find it easy or difficult to pray? What kind of spiritual books, other than the Bible, do you read? How often do you read the Bible?

Networking: Do you connect what you are doing with other men, for example, resources you come across at work? In other words, do you share contacts, know-how, resources, etc. with your male colleagues, friends, or employees regarding work or perhaps, a hobby?

If Retired: What was the transition like from being employed to being retired? Had you planned sufficiently for retirement? Now that you are retired, what do you find most meaningful in your life? What, least interesting?

Ultimate Issues: What are your fears, anxieties, concerns, for example, getting older, health problems, losing control over your memory, etc.? What are your ultimate issues?

CHAPTER 1

1. See chapters one and nine of my book, *Free to Pray, Free to Love: Growing in Prayer and Compassion* for a fuller description of my life before I joined the Jesuit Order. Available from Ave Maria Press, Notre Dame, IN, 1994.

2. The Jesuit novitiate is a two-year probationary period prior to taking vows of poverty, chastity, and obedience. During the novitiate, a novice makes a thirty-day retreat following the Spiritual Exercises of St. Ignatius of Loyola, the founder of the Society of Jesus (Jesuits). The novice supplements a variety of classes on the Jesuit way of life with regular household chores and opportunities to serve those who are economically poor or physically ill.

3. Francis Thompson, "The Hound of Heaven" (Wilton, CT: Morehouse-Barlow Co., Inc., 1980 edition), pp. 4-6.

4. Ibid., p. 26.

5. Nicholas Harnan, M.S.C., *The Heart's Journey Home: A Quest for Wisdom* (Notre Dame, IN: Ave Maria Press, 1992), pp. 32-43.

6. Stratford Sherman, "Leaders Learn to Heed the Voice Within," *Fortune Magazine* (August 22, 1994), p. 98.

7. *W.B. Yeats: Selected Poetry*, ed. by A. Norman Jeffares (London,: Pan Books, 1962), p. 16.

8. Jean-Pierre De Caussade, S.J., *The Joy of Full Surrender,* ed. by Hal M. Helms (Orleans, MA: Paraclete Press, 1986), p. 156. This quote is from the section of the book called, "Trials Connected With the State of Full Surrender." The book is a revised translation of the French classic *Abandonment to Divine Providence.*

9. Quoted at the beginning of the book, *Shadows of the Heart,* by Jim and Evelyn Whitehead (New York,: Crossroad Publishing Company, 1994).

10. Sam Keen, *Fire in the Belly: On Being a Man* (New York,: Bantam Books, 1991), pp. 127-128.

11. See George Aschenbrenner, S.J.'s article, "Consciousness Examen," *Review for Religious* (January, 1972). Also see Joseph A. Tetlow, S.J., "The Most Postmodern Prayer: American Jesuit Identity and the Examen of Conscience, 1920-1990," in *Studies in the Spirituality of Jesuits* (January 1994), especially the section, "The Masculine Energies," pp. 51-60, where the author discusses two male archetypes, the King and the Warrior, in relation to the Examen. (Available from: The Seminar on Jesuit Spirituality, 3700 West Pine Blvd., St. Louis, MO 63108).

12. William Johnston, S.J., *Being in Love: The Practice of Christian Prayer* (San Francisco: Harper and Row, 1989), pp. 122-128. See also chapter three of *How Can I Help? Stories and Reflections on Service,* by Ram Dass and Paul Gorman (New York: Alfred A. Knopf, 1985), especially the prayer exercise, "Opening to Pain," which is an aid to dissolving the boundaries we put up to try to block acceptance of our pain. The reader will also find helpful meditations in the book, *Wellsprings: A Book of Spiritual Exercises,* by Anthony de Mello, S.J. (Garden City, NY: Image Books). Of special note to the topic of suffering are "The Darkness," "The Revelation," "The King," "The Promise," "The Redemption," and "The Current."

13. Ibid., p. 122.

14. Ibid., p. 125.

15. T.S. Eliot, *Four Quartets* (New York: A Harvest Book, Harcourt, Brace and World, Inc., 1943), p. 32.

16. Marriage Encounter is designed to give married couples the opportunity to examine their lives together: their weaknesses and their strengths; their attitudes towards their families; their hurts, desires, ambitions, joys and frustrations. Couples share openly and honestly in a private, face-to-face, heart-to-heart "encounter" with the person with whom they have chosen to spend the rest of their life. Marriage Encounter was developed in the mid-1950's in Spain. The movement has spread through much of Europe and into the United States, and is non-denominational.

CHAPTER 2

1. Robert Moore and Douglas Gillette, *King, Warrior, Magician, Lover: Rediscovering the Archetypes of the Mature Masculine* (San Francisco: HarperCollins, 1990). See also Patrick Arnold's book, *Wildmen, Warriors, and Kings: Masculine Spirituality and the Bible* (New York: The Crossroad Publishing Company, 1991). The four basic feminine archetypes of the mature female are, according to Jungian analyst, Toni Wolff: Mother, Mediatrix, Companion, and Amazon. Amazon refers to how a woman manages her outer world. See Tad and Noreen Monroe Guzie's book, *About Men and Women: How Your Masculine and Feminine Archetypes Shape Your Destiny* (Mahwah, NJ: Paulist Press, 1986).

2. Robert A. Johnson, *She: Understanding Feminine Psychology* (New York: Harper and Row, 1989), p. 14. See also Johnson's excellent treatment of the archetypes and the unconscious in his book, *Inner Work Using Dreams and Active Imagination for Personal Growth* (San Francisco: Harper and Row, 1986), Section I.

3. Encyclopedia Britannica, Volume I, p. 489.

4. Robert G. Waldron, *Thomas Merton in Search of His Soul: A Jungian Perspective* (Notre Dame, IN: Ave Maria Press, 1994), p. 144.

5. Anne Brennan and Janice Brewi, *Celebrate Mid-Life: Jungian Archetypes and Mid-Life Spirituality* (New York: The Crossroad Publishing Company, 1988), p. 51.

6. See chapter five of my book, *Free to Pray, Free to Love: Growing in Prayer and Compassion* for a fuller explanation of this mode of the intuitive way of thinking. Also see Frances E. Vaughan, *Awakening Intuition* (Garden City, NY: Anchor Books, 1979) for both an excellent explanation of intuition and some practical exercises geared to help the intuitive to emerge more fully.

7. Moore and Gillette, p. 10.

8. I wish to acknowledge three primary sources for my understanding of the shadow: Dr. Diana Greg, a psychotherapist, who practices in San Diego, California, William A. Miller, and Robert A. Johnson.

9. Johnson, p. 25.

10. See chapter two of *Free to Pray, Free to Love* for a fuller explanation of this prayer and some of the effects of it on my life. I have shared the Freedom Prayer on numerous retreats. People continually relate to me the effectiveness that praying this way has had in their lives.

11. Dr. Diana Greg, unpublished reflections.

12. There are many excellent books written on dream analysis. One that has been especially helpful to me is *The Dream Game,* by Ann Faraday (New York: Harper and Row, 1974). In terms of the shadow, see especially chapter eleven.

13. William A. Miller, *Make Friends with Your Shadow: How to Accept and Use Positively the Negative Side of Your Personality* (Minneapolis, MN: Augsburg Publishing House, 1981), p. 127. See also John Sanford, *Evil, the Shadow Side of Reality* (New York: The Crossroad Publishing Company, 1992) and Robert A. Johnson, *Owning Your Own Shadow* (San Francisco: HarperCollins, 1991).

CHAPTER 3

1. Moore and Gillette, p. 59.

2. Ibid., pp. 61-62.

3. Richard Rohr, OFM, *Quest for the Grail* (New York: The Crossroad Publishing Company, 1994), p. 57.

4. Moore and Gillette, pp. 64-65. A powerful, fictional, account of father-mother wounds can be found in the book, *The Prince of Tides,* by Pat Conroy (New York: Bantam Books, Paperback Edition, 1986).

CHAPTER 4

1. The feminine counterpart is the Amazon. According to Christina Spahn ("Images of the Feminine," an article from the periodical, *Radical Grace,* August-September, 1991), the Amazon is independent and self-contained. She finds her identity and fulfillment in managing the outside world. She is clearly focused, zealous, and energetic, is inspired by competition, efficient and organized. She can be mature or immature just as the Warrior can be true or false.

2. Moore and Gillette, p. 79.

3. Ibid., p. 80.

4. Peter Kreeft, *Making Sense Out of Suffering* (Ann Arbor, MI: Servant Books, 1986), pp. 63-65.

5. Jamie Sams and David Carson, *Medicine Cards* (Santa Fe, N.M: Bear and Company, 1988), p. 49.

6. Ibid., p. 49.

7. I am indebted to Richard Rohr for his presentation of the structure of the mythical Hero (or Heroine's) journey, as developed by the late Joseph Campbell, some of which I have adapted for my own conferences. I present it here because it is an excellent tool for self-reflection and for fuller appreciation of the function of the Warrior archetype in the inner journey. See Joseph Campbell's landmark work, *The Hero with a Thousand Faces* (New York: MJF Books, 1949).

8. See my book, *Free to Pray, Free to Love,* Chapter Six, for a fuller explanation of the spiritual dark nights.

9. The Spiritual Exercises of St. Ignatius of Loyola, a classic retreat manual in the Roman Catholic tradition, is four hundred years old. It sprang from the rich mystical experiences and the dynamic spiritual principles with which God gifted Ignatius. For a modern translation see, David Fleming, S.J., *The Spiritual Exercises of St. Ignatius: A Literal Translation and A Contemporary Reading* (St. Louis, MO: The Institute of Jesuit Sources, 1978; 3700 West Pine Blvd., Saint Louis, Missouri 63108). The retreat is usually made over an eight- or thirty-day period, though it is also possible to present the key themes on a weekend retreat. The prayer, *Anima Christi*, can be found on p. 3 of this book.

10. Jean-Pierre De Caussade, *The Joy of Full Surrender* (Orleans, MA: Paraclete Press, 1986), p.157.

11. T. S. Eliot, *Four Quartets* (New York,: A Harvest Book, Harcourt, Brace and World, Inc., 1943), p. 59.

12. Moore and Gillette, pp. 87-88.

13. Patrick Arnold, *Wildmen, Warriors, and Kings: Masculine Spirituality and the Bible* (New York: The Crossroad Publishing Co., 1991).

14. Ibid., p. 104.

15. Richard Rohr, OFM, *Quest for the Grail*, p. 94.

16. Michael Cavanagh, *Make Your Tomorrow Better* (Mahwah, NJ: Paulist Press), p. 68. Chapter Three is on fear, the basic emotion. Besides describing various basic fears, the author offers a variety of ways to deal with them.

17. Stratford Sherman, "Leaders Learn to Heed the Voice Within," *Fortune Magazine* (August 22, 1994), pp. 98 & 100. Two excellent additional resources for this chapter are Frank R. Podgorski's article, "Joseph Cambell's Catholic Vision," (*Human Development,* Fall 1990), pp. 40-46 and "The Grail Quest: Male Spirituality," by William J. O'Malley (*America,* May 9, 1992), pp. 402-406.

CHAPTER 5

1. Moore and Gillette, p. 110.

2. Ibid., p.98.

3. For further information on Promise Keepers contact: National Office, P.O. Box 18376, Boulder, Colorado 80308 (800-888-7595).

4. Moore and Gillette, p. 103.

5. Pierre Teilhard de Chardin, *Let Me Explain,* texts selected and arranged by Jean-Pierre Demoulin (New York: Harper and Row, 1970), p.42.

6. See, *Free to Pray, Free to Love: Growing in Prayer and Compassion,* p.122. This is from Chapter Eight, "Compassion for the Earth."

7. See pages 125-126 book *Free to Pray, Free to Love,* for some additional prayer exercises that can be done in nature.

8. Wilferd A. Peterson, *The Art of Living* (New York: Simon and Schuster, 1961), pp. 18-19.

9. Quoted in my book, *Praying the Beatitudes: A Retreat on the Sermon on the Mount* (Dublin, Ireland: Veritas, 1990; distributed in the United States by Ignatius Press), p.60. This is from the Beatitude, "Blessed are they who hunger and thirst for justice . . ."

10. Richard Rohr, OFM, *Quest for the Grail,* p. 149.

11. For a more thorough treatment of the true self, see Chapter Nine of *Free to Pray, Free to Love.* Basically, the true self is that part of me that really believes I am loved by God and therefore wants to do what God wants; the false self does not believe and thus does not want to do what God asks.

12. Thomas Merton, *New Seeds of Contemplation* (New York: A New Directions Book, 1961), pp. 35-36.

13. For a reflective consideration of how to clarify one's identity, see Chapter One of *Free to Pray, Free to Love,* "The Unconditional Love of God."

14. *America's Fascinating Indian Heritage* (Pleasantville, NY: The Reader's Digest Association, Inc., 1978), p.143. This process is not just for the young. It is never too late for inner progress. I experienced what I would call a

midlife Vision Quest (going in the direction of my fear for greater wholeness) at the age of 57.

15. Patrick M. Arnold, *Wildmen, Warriors, and Kings: Masculine Spirituality and the Bible* (New York: Crossroad, 1991), p.108.

16. Jaimie Sams and David Carson, *Medicine Cards: The Discovery of Power Through the Ways of Animals* (Santa Fe, New Mexico: Bear and Company, 1988), p.101. The book explores intuition through identification with our connections to various animals.

17. Ibid., p.101.

18. Ibid., p.102.

19. By Ken Eckel, retired, husband, father of five grown children.

20. By George Appleton.

21. John D. Campos, who is twenty-nine years old.

22. Pierre Teilhard de Chardin, *The Divine Milieu* (New York: Harper and Row, 1960), pp.76-77.

23. Arnold, p. 158, taken from his chapter, "Jonah the Trickster."

24. Dave Barry, *Dave Barry's Complete Guide to Guys* (New York: Random House, 1995), pp.xx-xxi.

25. Peterson, p.16. From *The Art of Living*.

26. Ake Hultkrantz, *The Religions of the American Indians* (Berkeley, CA: U. of California Press, 1967), pp.34-35. Another good resource on the Trickster is the journal *Parabola* (Myth and the Quest for Meaning), Volume IV, No. 1, February, 1979.

27. Achilles was the greatest Greek warrior in the Trojan War and hero of Homer's Iliad. He killed Hector and was killed when Paris wounded him in the heel, his one vulnerable spot, with an arrow.

28. Bill Moyers interview of Joseph Campbell. Titled *The Power of Myth*, it is available on six audio cassettes published by Highbridge Company, 1000 Westgate Drive, St. Paul, Minnesota 55114.

29. Co-dependency studies originated with alcoholism. However, one can experience this problem in other circumstances. An excellent resource is Melody Beattie's book, *Co-Dependent No More* (Hazelden Foundation, 1987). She not only describes the characteristics of co-dependency, but also suggests ways to combat it.

30. Dom Bede Griffiths, *The Marriage of East and West* (Springfield, IL: Templegate Publishers, 1982), pp.151-152. An excellent resource on the teachings of Dom Bede is, *The Other Half of My Soul: Bede Griffiths and the*

Hindu-Christian Dialogue, edited and compiled by Beatrice Bruteau (Quest Books: The Theosophical Publishing House, P.O. Box 270, Wheaton, Illinois 60189-0270).

31. Moore and Gillette, p. 118.

32. See Frances E. Vaughan's excellent book, *Awakening Intuition* (Garden City, NY: Anchor Books, 1979). The author guides the reader to a greater realization of one's intuitive powers through suggested exercises. She treats dream analysis, creativity, and practical problem-solving. Also see Part Four of Bede Griffiths' book (cf. note 30). The chapter is titled, "The Way of Intuitive Wisdom." See Chapter Five of *Free to Pray, Free to Love,* on "Intuition and Prayer" and pages 113-120, "Intuition, Compassion, and Justice."

CHAPTER 6

1. Jesuit Father Pierre Teilhard de Chardin wrote many books, of particular interest for the Lover archetype see, *The Divine Milieu* (Harper Torch Books, 1960) and *Hymn of the Universe* (Harper Torch Books, 1965).

2. Moore and Gillette, p. 120.

3. Ibid., p. 120.

4. See chapter one of my book, *Free to Pray, Free to Love,* for a fuller treatment of this important facet of our faith life. A biblical reference to this reality of God's love for us can be found, in mystical terms, in the Song of Songs.

5. Kathleen R. Fischer and Thomas N. Hart, *Promises to Keep: Developing the Skills of Marriage* (Mahwah, NJ: Paulist Press, 1991), pp. 14-16.

6. See Ken Wilber's book, Eye to Eye: *The Quest for the New Paradigm,* pp. 90-91, for an informative description on the dynamic of repression (Anchor Books, 1983).

7. See chapter two of *Free to Pray, Free to Love,* especially pages 31-37.

8. *Free to Pray, Free to Love,* p. 80.

9. James Nelson, Ph.D., "Masculine Sexuality and Masculine Spirituality," *SIECUS* Report (March 1985), p. 4. SIECUS stands for The Sex Information and Education Council of the U.S.

10. Moore and Gillette, pp. 140-141.

11. Daniel Day Williams, *The Spirit and the Forms of Love* (New York: Harper and Row, 1968), p. 216. This quotation is in Chapter XI, "Love and Sexuality".

12. Taken from *Christopher News Notes,* No. 269, May 1983. This issue titled, "Human Sexuality: A Perspective."

13. Ben Swagerty of Roseburg, Oregon.

14. The author wishes to remain anonymous.

15. See *Breach of Trust, Breach of Faith: Child Sexual Abuse in the Church and Society*, by the Canadian Conference of Catholic Bishops, 1992 (90 Parent Ave., Ottawa K1N 7B1), p. C-1. This is a workbook of materials for discussion groups.

16. *Free to Pray, Free to Love*, p. 146.

17. Bernadette Kimmerling, "Sexual Love and the Love of God: A Spirituality of Sexuality," *Doctrine and Life* (A four part series, 1986), pp. 302-303. From Part I. *Doctrine and Life* is published in Ireland by Dominican Publications, 42 Parnell Square, Dublin 1.

18. This pamphlet is available for purchase in quantities of 50 or more. To order or for pricing information, call toll-free 1-800-321-4407 or write ETR Associates, P.O. Box 1830, Santa Cruz, California 95061-1830. Title #063.

19. Nelson, p. 3.

20. Ibid., p. 3

21. Ibid., p. 4

22. Mary Ellen Ashcroft and Holly Bridges ed., *Bearing Our Sorrows* Elliot (San Francisco: HarperCollins, 1993), p. 51.

CHAPTER 7

1. "A Gathering of Men." with Bill Moyers and Robert Bly (Public Affairs Television, Inc., 1990). The transcript is available from, Journal Graphics, Inc., 267 Broadway, New York, N.Y. 10007.

2. Ibid., p. 8.

3. Ibid., p. 4.

4. Dr. Alan D. Wolfelt, "Gender Roles and Grief: Why Men's Grief Is Naturally Complicated," *Thanatos* (Fall, 1990), p. 21.

5. For further insight on father wounds and grieving over them, see Chapter Three, "The Road of Ashes, Descent, and Grief," in Robert Bly's book, *Iron John: A Book About Men* (New York: Addison-Wesley Publishing Company, Inc., 1990). This book is sometimes difficult to interpret because it is an allegory. I suggest reading an introductory book to the field of masculine psychology first, for example, *Fire in the Belly: On Being a Man*, by Sam Keen (New York: Bantam Books, 1991). I found this book an excellent introduction to the topic.

6. Quoted in *Iron John: A Book About Men*, p. 76.

7. Two books in particular were helpful in my journey: *Wildmen, Warriors, and Kings: Masculine Spirituality and the Bible* by Patrick Arnold, S.J. (New York: Crossroad Publishing Co., 1991) and *Fire in the Belly: On Being a Man* by Sam Keen (New York: Bantam Books, 1991).

8. *Iron John: A Book About Men*, p. 88. For an additional resource on grieving, see Chapter Two, "Blessed are the Sorrowing; They Shall be Consoled" from my book, *Praying the Beatitudes: A Retreat on the Sermon on the Mount.*

CHAPTER 8

1. George Aschenbrenner, S.J., "Consciousness Examen," *Review for Religious* (January, 1972; Address: 3601 Lindell Blvd., St. Louis, Missouri 63108-3393). This is the basic source I am using for this reflective exercise. See also *Experiencing God in Daily Life,* by Robert Fabing, S.J. (North American Liturgy Resources, 1989; 10802 North 23rd Avenue, Phoenix, Arizona 85029).

2. Aschenbrenner, p. 17.

3. Ibid., p. 16.

4. Ibid., p. 16.

5. Ira Progoff, *At a Journal Workshop: The Basic Text and Guide for Using the Intensive Journal* (New York: Dialogue House Library, 1976).

6. Max Oliva, S.J., "Developing a Christian Social Conscience," *Review for Religious* (July-August, 1983).

7. Thomas Moore, *Care of the Soul: A Guide for Cultivating Depth and Sacredness in Everyday Life* (New York: HarperCollins,1992).

8. The original printed source of these suggestions could not be found.

FINAL WORD

1. Chapter one. See also Joseph F. Schmidt's book, *Praying Our Experiences* (Winona, MN: St. Mary's Press, 1989), *The Seasons of a Man's Life*, by Daniel Levinson (New York: Ballantine Books, 1978), and *What Are They Saying About Masculine Spirituality?* by David C. James (Mahwah, NJ: Paulist Press, 1996).

2. Abraham Joshua Heschel, *Who Is Man?* (Stanford,CA: Stanford UP, 1955), p. 36.

Fr. Max Oliva (r) with "Uncle" Bob Smith.

Fr. Max Oliva, a Jesuit priest living in San Diego, California, has been conducting retreats, seminars, and workshops on spirituality since 1974. He has given retreats throughout the U.S., in Canada, Ireland, and South Africa, and frequently leads retreats for men's groups. Fr. Oliva is also the author of *Praying the Beatitudes* and *Free to Pray, Free to Love* (Ave Maria Press).